MATT AND TOM OLDFIELD

ULTIMATE
FOOTBALL HEROES

VAN DIJK

FROM THE PLAYGROUND
TO THE PITCH

DINO

First published by Dino Books in 2019,
An imprint of Bonnier Books UK,
The Plaza,
535 Kings Road,
London SW10 0SZ

@dinobooks
@footieheroesbks
www.heroesfootball.com
www.bonnierbooks.co.uk

Text © Matt Oldfield 2019
The right of Matt Oldfield to be identified as the author of this work has been
asserted by him in accordance with the copyright, designs and patents act 1988.

Design by www.envydesign.co.uk

Paperback ISBN: 9781789461206
E-book ISBN: 9781789461831

British Library cataloguing-in-publication data:
A catalogue record for this book is available from the British Library.

Printed and bound in Great Britain by Clays Lltd, Elcograf S.p.A.

1 3 5 7 9 10 8 6 4 2

For Iona, Katie, Ian, Naomi, Barny,
Beckie, Rob and Dion Dublin

ULTIMATE
FOOTBALL HEROES

Matt Oldfield is an accomplished writer and the editor-in-chief
of football review site *Of Pitch & Page*. Tom Oldfield is a freelance
sports writer and the author of biographies on Cristiano Ronaldo,
Arsène Wenger and Rafael Nadal.

Cover illustration by Dan Leydon.
To learn more about Dan visit danleydon.com
To purchase his artwork visit etsy.com/shop/footynews
Or just follow him on Twitter @danleydon

TABLE OF CONTENTS

ACKNOWLEDGEMENTS

First of all, I'd like to thank Bonnier Books UK – and particularly my editor Laura Pollard – for supporting me throughout and running the ever-expanding UFH ship so smoothly. Writing stories for the next generation of football fans is both an honour and a pleasure.

I wouldn't be doing this if it wasn't for my brother Tom. I owe him so much and I'm very grateful for his belief in me as an author. I feel like Robin setting out on a solo career after a great partnership with Batman. I hope I do him (Tom, not Batman) justice with these new books.

Next up, I want to thank my friends for keeping

me sane during long hours in front of the laptop.
Pang, Will, Mills, Doug, John, Charlie – the laughs
and the cups of coffee are always appreciated.

I've already thanked my brother but I'm also very
grateful to the rest of my family, especially Melissa,
Noah and of course Mum and Dad. To my parents, I
owe my biggest passions: football and books. They're
a real inspiration for everything I do.

Finally, I couldn't have done this without Iona's
encouragement and understanding during long,
work-filled weekends. Much love to you.

CHAPTER 1

EUROPEAN CHAMPION!

1 June 2019, Wanda Metropolitano Stadium, Madrid

For Virgil and his Liverpool teammates, it felt great to be back in the Champions League Final for the second year in a row. Last time, they had lost 3–1 to Cristiano Ronaldo's Real Madrid; this time, only a win would do.

Liverpool! Liverpool! Liverpool!

Although the location had changed, from Ukraine to Spain, the electric atmosphere in the stadium had stayed the same. That's because the Liverpool fans were the best in the world, and they had plenty to cheer about, especially after the 'Miracle of Anfield'.

terrific team had fought back from 3–0 down in the semi-final first leg, to beat Lionel Messi's Barcelona 4–3! Now, with a victory over their Premier League rivals Tottenham, they could lift the trophy and become Champions of Europe for the sixth time.

Liverpool! Liverpool! Liverpool!

'Are you ready, big man?' the manager Jürgen Klopp asked his star centre-back as the players left the dressing room before kick-off.

Virgil didn't say a word; he didn't need to. Instead, he just gave his manager a confident nod. Oh yes, he was ready and raring to go! Big games called for big game players, and he was the ultimate big game player. That's why Liverpool had paid £75 million to sign him from Southampton, making him the most expensive defender in the world. He was always so calm and composed. He never got nervous and he loved playing under pressure. He was born for this – the biggest stage in club football.

'Right, lads,' their captain Jordan Henderson called out from the front of the Liverpool line. 'It's time to go out there and win the Champions League!'

'YEAH!' the other ten players cheered behind him:

Alisson,

Joël Matip,

Andy Robertson,

Trent Alexander-Arnold,

Gini Wijnaldum,

Fabinho,

Roberto Firmino,

Sadio Mané,

Mohamed Salah,

and in the middle, the man at the centre of everything – Virgil!

What a talented team, and their spirit was so strong too. After the 'Miracle of Anfield', the Liverpool players felt like they could achieve absolutely anything. They were all fired up and determined to put their previous disappointments behind them – losing the 2018 Champions League Final to Real Madrid, and also losing the 2019 Premier League title to Manchester City. That one still hurt badly, but a European trophy would help make them feel a whole lot better. This was their moment to bring glory back to Liverpool Football Club.

As he waited in the tunnel, Virgil casually reached up a long arm to touch the ceiling above him, just like he did with the 'This is Anfield' sign back home. He liked to tap it for good luck, not that they would need any of that...

When the big moment arrived, Virgil walked slowly out onto the pitch in Madrid, straight past the Champions League trophy without even looking at it.

'That can wait until it's ours to keep!' he told himself.

Virgil wasn't messing around. In the very first minute, he muscled his way past Tottenham's star striker Harry Kane to win the ball. He headed it down to Gini, who passed to Jordan, who lifted it over the top for Sadio to chase. The Liverpool attack looked so dangerous already. And as Sadio tried to chip the ball back to Jordan, it struck the Spurs midfielder Moussa Sissoko on the arm.

'Handball!' cried Sadio.

'Handball!' cried Virgil, way back in defence.

The referee pointed to the spot. *Penalty!*

Mohamed stepped up and... scored – *1–0!*

What a perfect start! Virgil jogged over to join in the team celebrations but then it was straight back to business. When there was defending to do, he was Liverpool's leader, organising everyone around him.

'That's your man, Joël!'

'Close him down, Gini!'

'Watch that run, Robbo!'

'Stay focused, Trent!'

'Come on guys, this isn't over yet!'

Virgil loved talking, and he spoke from experience. Once upon a time, he had been a talented young defender who made too many mistakes, but not anymore. He had learnt so many harsh lessons during his years with Willem II, Groningen, Celtic, Southampton and the Netherlands national team. And each one had helped to make him an even better, smarter footballer.

At half-time, Liverpool still had their 1–0 lead. They were now just forty-five minutes away from Champions League glory...

'Come on lads, keep fighting!' Klopp urged his tired players. 'One more, final push!'

It was the end of a very long season, but Virgil wasn't going to head off on his summer holidays empty-handed. No way, this trophy belonged to Liverpool! He fought hard for every header and tackle, and he won them all.

He's a centre-half, he's a number four,
Watch him defend, and watch him score,
He'll pass the ball, calm as you like,
He's Virgil van Dijk, he's Virgil van Dijk!

Tottenham weren't giving up, though. As Dele Alli played a quick pass forward to Son Heung-min, they had two vs. two in attack. Joël was marking Kane, which meant that it was Virgil's job to stop Son Heung-min.

No problem! The South Korean had lots of speed and skill, but so did Virgil. He was the complete centre-back and not one Premier League striker had got past him all season. He knew exactly what to do in these difficult situations...

Virgil followed Son all the way into the Liverpool penalty area, keeping up but never diving in. He wasn't that kind of a defender. Instead, Virgil waited patiently and cleverly until the crucial moment. Then he used his strength and long legs to clear the ball away for a corner-kick.

'Phew!' the Liverpool fans breathed a big sigh of relief. Virgil had saved the day yet again!

'Great work!' shouted Alisson, patting him on the back.

'Keep going!' shouted Virgil, clapping encouragingly towards his teammates.

There were still fifteen minutes to go, and a second Liverpool goal would really help to calm things down. What could Virgil do to help his attackers at the other end of the field? He sliced his shot in the Tottenham penalty area, but then battled to win the second ball. Virgil's flick-on landed at Joël's feet, who set up super sub Divock Origi to score. 2–0!

As the goal went in, Virgil was racing back

into defence. He turned and threw his arms up triumphantly. What would Liverpool do without him? He had played his part yet again. Now, they just had to hold on…

At last, the final whistle blew – Liverpool were the new Champions of Europe! Virgil didn't jump for joy like many of his teammates; instead, he fell to the floor. The exhaustion, the emotion, the excitement – at first, it was all too much for him to take. He had been dreaming about this moment since he was six years old. Was he still dreaming? No, it was real!

Virgil didn't stay down on the grass for long. His teammates wouldn't let him.

'We did it! We did it!' Gini Wijnaldum shouted, high-fiving his friend.

'Yes, Virg!' Alisson cheered, wrapping him in a big bear hug.

With tears in his eyes and the Anfield roar ringing in his ears, Virgil walked proudly around the pitch. He was a Champions League winner now. 'Champions League winner' – yes, he liked the sound of that.

'I told you we'd win it!' Virgil told his manager as they embraced near the halfway line.

After lots of hugs and high-fives, it was time for the Liverpool players to collect their winners' medals and then, best of all, the trophy! As Jordan the captain lifted the cup high above his head, flames shot up around the stage. Virgil, of course, was at the back of the team huddle, towering over everyone and cheering at the top of his voice:

Campeones, Campeones, Olé! Olé! Olé!

What a feeling! One by one, Virgil was achieving all his childhood football dreams. First, he had become the new captain of the Netherlands national team and now, the Boy from Breda was a European Champion too.

CHAPTER 2

BOY FROM BREDA

Hellen van Dijk had four important life lessons that she wanted to pass on to her children:

Be respectful.

Work hard.

Stay positive.

Always follow your dreams.

For her eldest son Virgil, those dreams were all about becoming a professional football player. It had been his favourite sport since the very first time he kicked a ball. It was the only thing he ever talked about, and the only thing he wanted to do, all day, every day. At the age of six, he was already out there on the local pitches, battling for the ball and battling to be the best.

'Pass it!'

'Hey, that's a foul!'

'Goooooaaaaaallllllll!'

Virgil was far from the only youngster with those superstar dreams, however. Football was the most popular sport in the Netherlands, where he lived, and also across the whole, wide world. So, the road to the top would be a long and winding one, especially for a boy from Breda.

Breda was a city in the south of the Netherlands, more famous for its factories than for its football stars. Although they did have a local team, NAC Breda, they played down in the Dutch second division. To Virgil, the big clubs like Ajax and Feyenoord felt a long, long way away. He didn't really have many local football heroes to look up to, other than the big kids who showed off their skills on the pitches near where they lived.

Most of the best Dutch footballers either came from big cities in the north of the country:

Dennis Bergkamp, Johan Cruyff, Marco van Basten, Frank and Ronald de Boer…

Or, their families had moved to the Netherlands from a small country in South America called Suriname:

Patrick Kluivert, Edgar Davids, Clarence Seedorf, Aron Winter, Frank Rijkaard, Ruud Gullit...

And Virgil's mum! Yes, Hellen was from Suriname too, just like Seedorf and Davids! Sadly, she didn't have enough money to take her children on the long flight back to visit her birthplace. So instead, from their home in Breda, she taught them as much as she could about the history and culture of the country.

'We Surinamese like to stay calm and enjoy life,' she joked with Virgil. 'We're not as uptight as Dutch people like your dad!'

'Hey, I heard that!' Ron replied with a smile.

'Good!' Hellen laughed, before moving on to her son's favourite subject. 'And when it comes to football, our players have got it all – power, pace, and of course, that South American skill. No, you don't find that kind of natural talent in the Netherlands!'

At first having parents from different countries made Virgil feel a bit different from his friends, both

those at school and on the pitch. But the older he
grew, the prouder he became of his background. The
Netherlands and Suriname – like all those football
heroes before him, he was determined to bring
together the best of both worlds.

CHAPTER 3

WDS'19

When Virgil arrived at his first training session with his local youth team in Breda, WDS'19, the coaches asked him the usual question: what position do you like to play?

'Striker,' he replied without even pausing to think.

Like most seven-year-old footballers, Virgil thought scoring goals was way cooler than stopping them.

The powerful feeling of ball hitting boot,

BANG!

The awesome sight of it flying past the keeper and into the net,

ZOOM!

And, best of all, the roar of the crowd celebrating your huge hero moment.

HURRAAAAAAY!

What could be better than that? Definitely not
blocking other people's shots, that's for sure!
Shooting or tackling – was that question even worth
asking?! Not to young Virgil – he knew which one
he preferred.

'Remember, the goalscorers get all the glory,' he
taught his younger brother, who was learning fast
about football. Soon, he'd be ready to go in goal and
face Virgil's fierce shots. 'That's why the best players
are always attackers.'

Virgil was aiming to become the next Ronaldinho,
not the next Paolo Maldini. The Brazilian was always
smiling and always trying out exciting new tricks.
Virgil loved watching skilful players who looked like
they were having lots of fun. To him, that's what
football was all about.

'OK, well let's see how you get on up front then,'
agreed Ferdi Hoogeboom, John van den Berg and
Rik Kleyn.

They were the three coaches in charge at WDS'19.
The first thing they noticed about Virgil – other than

his confidence – was his size. He was easily the tallest boy on the team, and once he started playing, easily the strongest too.

Virgil started the match in the striker's role, but he didn't stay there long. He wanted to be on the ball all the time, and he wasn't just going to wait for it to eventually arrive at his feet. He dropped deeper and deeper until he was in the middle of the field, at the centre of everything.

Then calmly and cleverly, Virgil took control of the game. He used his superior size and strength to win the ball back for his team, and then pushed his team forward with his dribbling and passing.

'He looks so comfortable on the ball,' van den Berg turned to Hoogeboom, sounding impressed. 'And he's not shy, is he, for a new kid?'

Virgil was organising everything, telling his teammates where to go and what to do.

'Luuk, make the run!'

'Bas, watch the left winger!'

'Come on guys, I'm marking two players here!'

Already, at the age of seven, this kid was clearly a

leader. And he was clearly a defender or midfielder – not an attacker.

'Why do kids always say they're strikers?' Hoogeboom, van den Berg and Kleyn laughed together, rolling their eyes. 'Is that the only position they've heard of?!'

The WDS'19 coaches were delighted with their new young signing, and so were the players. Suddenly, the goalkeeper had hardly any saves to make, and the other defenders didn't need to panic anymore – because, if their opponents did get through, Virgil was always there to save the day. No-one got past Virgil – no-one. He wasn't the quickest player, but it didn't matter. He was really good at reading the game and working out what the striker would do next.

'He plays like a little professional already!' Kleyn thought to himself.

Virgil loved every minute of every WDS match. He was actually quite happy about not being the striker because it meant he got to be more involved in the action – the passing, the tackling, the battling for the ball. Maybe he would be the next Maldini after all, or the next Edgar Davids in midfield. He would just have to save all his great goalscoring for kickarounds with friends.

Virgil wore his blue-and-white shirt with passion and pride. He was playing for a proper team now, with his own special shirt number on the back, just like his heroes. It felt like the first step on his journey to the top. WDS had links with the local professional football club, NAC Breda, and then after that? Who knew! Well, Virgil had a plan, of course.

'One day, I'm going to play in a Champions League final,' he told his dad excitedly as they drove home together after another WDS win, 'and I'll be the captain of the Netherlands national team too!'

CHAPTER 4

KING OF THE
CRUYFF COURT

Virgil's life was all about football. When he wasn't
playing the game, he was still thinking about playing
it, and imagining how it would feel to be a famous
superstar in the future.

'Don't worry, I'll buy us a big, big house,' he
promised his mum, 'and lots of fast, fancy cars too!'

Virgil didn't have a lot of time for thinking,
however, because he was too busy playing. There
was always a game going on somewhere, a chance
to practise his skills. When he wasn't training or
winning matches for WDS, he was taking shot
after shot against his brother in the big goals near
their house until it got dark. Or even better, he was

winning matches on the local Cruyff court.

The pitches were named after Johan Cruyff, the greatest Dutch player of all time. In 2003, his charity had opened courts all over the country to give young kids a space to call their own where they could play football. There were two courts in Breda, and one of them was very near to where the van Dijks lived. It was a small pitch, covered in short, artificial grass, and surrounded by a high, wire fence to stop balls from flying out into the roads or through neighbours' windows. During most evenings, weekends and school holidays, that Cruyff court was Virgil's home.

'Do you want to take a sleeping bag with you?' Ron joked as his son rushed out of the door.

Virgil couldn't reply because he was still eating his breakfast, so he just waved goodbye instead.

'Well, at least we know where to find him if we need him!' Hellen said to her husband with a smile. They were just happy to see their son outside, having fun, getting exercise and staying out of trouble.

Well, Virgil was staying out of trouble off the football pitch anyway. The five-a-side games on the

Cruyff court were so competitive that there were often arguments and angry challenges. Although Virgil tried to stay away from the fighting, he was always fearless in the tackle. You had to be brave and confident if you wanted to keep playing. Most days, there was a tournament with lots of different teams and it was 'winner stays on'. If you lost, you had to wait ages on the sidelines before it was your turn again. No-one wanted that. They were too young to get tired; everyone just wanted to play football for as long as possible.

'Come on, let's do this!'

On the Cruyff court, Virgil wasn't a defender or a midfielder. He was usually one of the younger kids there, and so, unlike at WDS, he was smaller and weaker than the others. Instead, he played on the wing or in attack, where he could try out all his Ronaldinho tricks.

The aim of the game was to win, but also to out-skill your opponent – the cooler the move, the louder the cheer from the crowd. Providing entertainment was key, especially with so many people watching.

There wasn't much space on the small Cruyff court, though, and the level of football was always really high. Sometimes, professional players from NAC Breda would even come down for a bit of extra training. So Virgil's first touch had to be really good, and his fancy footwork had to be really fast. Practice made perfect.

'Skills, Virg!'

'Woah, Jordy will never come back after you embarrassed him like that!'

Virgil enjoyed his fun Cruyff Court battles, and he learned a lot from them. After all, quick thinking and close control were really useful weapons on a bigger, eleven-a-side pitch too.

As Virgil grew older – and taller and stronger – he was making a name for himself as one of the best young players in Breda. But could he go on from being King of the Cruyff Court to become a football legend and the future captain of the Netherlands national team?

They were big dreams to have, but Virgil believed in himself.

CHAPTER 5

A WARM WELCOME AT WILLEM II

The next step in Virgil's football career was a trial at the top local team. The pressure to perform well made some of the young players panic, but not Virgil. He was as calm and confident as ever as his dad dropped him off at the NAC Breda training ground.

'Good luck!' Ron called through the car window.

'Thanks!'

Virgil was excited about the opportunity that lay ahead of him. If he did well at the trial, he might get the chance to move on from WDS to bigger and better things. He was going to work his way up to the top, one step at a time.

He understood that things would be more serious at a proper, professional football club like Breda, but the transition was still quite shocking to him.

'What are you doing?!' the youth coach yelled at his players. 'No, no, NO – you're getting it all *WRONG!*'

It was mostly silent during the session, and the Breda youngsters seemed very serious. Wasn't football supposed to be fun? The atmosphere was so different to WDS, where everyone enjoyed themselves and shouted encouragement at each other. Could Virgil see himself staying somewhere that was so different to WDS?

'So, how did it go?' Ron asked when he arrived to pick his son up.

Virgil knew it was best to tell the truth: 'Dad, it was horrible, I hated it!'

'I'm sorry it didn't suit you, son,' Ron comforted him. 'Don't worry, there are plenty of other football clubs around. We'll find the right one for you.'

The next week, they drove twenty miles to Tilburg, the home of Willem II.

'This team is even better than Breda,' Ron
explained on the journey. 'They finished second in
the Dutch League last season, ahead of Ajax and PSV.
And now, they're playing in the Champions League!'

Virgil's ears pricked up at the sound of those two
wonderful words. Wow, Willem II must be really
good if they were playing in the Champions League!
By the time they got to the training ground, Virgil
couldn't wait for the trial to start. He was ready to
shine at a Champions League club.

This time, there was no shouting from the coaches
as he arrived. Instead, there was a warm welcome
from the Willem II youth coach, Jan van Loon.

'Thanks for coming, Virgil – it's great to have
you here.'

Wow, what a difference! As he walked out onto
the training field, Virgil could tell that he was going
to like the atmosphere at Willem II. The players were
laughing and joking as they warmed up, and once
the session started, they worked hard while also
having fun. Much better!

'Excellent, Virgil!' van Loon clapped and cheered

when he stopped one of the strikers in a one-on-one situation.

The coach watched as Virgil won the ball again… and again… and again. The Willem strikers tried and tried, but no-one could get past the powerful new defender.

It wasn't just Virgil's strength that impressed van Loon; it was also his understanding of the game. Just when it looked like a striker was about to get past him, he would stretch out a leg and steal the ball at the crucial moment. Other players were quicker, but Virgil always seemed to know where to be, when to act and what to do next. He made it all look so easy, but it was very rare to see such a natural defender at such a young age.

'Some of that stuff can take years to teach!' van Loon thought to himself.

And some of it you couldn't teach at all; it was just instinct. You either had it, or you didn't, and Virgil definitely had it. The Willem II youth coach knew straight away that he had to sign this special talent.

'So, how did it go?' Ron asked at the end of the

session. He had been watching from the car with his fingers crossed because he didn't want to put his son off on his big day.

'Dad, this is Jan, the coach,' Virgil replied, trying to control the smile spreading across his face.

'Nice to meet you, Jan.'

'Nice to meet you too, Mr van Dijk.'

'Please, call me Ron.'

'Ron, I'll keep it short – your son has a very special talent! Our strikers spent ages trying to beat him today, but no-one managed it – not a single one. We'd love for Virgil to join us here at Willem II. We think with some extra coaching, he could be a real star. Would you like some time to think about it first?'

Ron looked across at Virgil, who was shaking his head violently. He didn't want to wait; he wanted to play for Willem straight away.

'No, I think my son has made up his mind already!' Ron laughed. 'Thanks, he'd love to join the team.'

CHAPTER 6

DISHWASHING DAYS

At first, Virgil moved smoothly through the ranks of the Willem II academy. He made each new age group look as easy as the last. With the right kind of coaching, he was developing into a top young defender. But things began to change when he reached the Under-17s.

Until then, Virgil had always been one of the biggest and strongest players on his team.

But now that he was sixteen, everyone else but him had grown. Even his younger brother was taller than him now! Virgil had to play at right-back instead because his coach didn't think he was fast enough, or good enough, to be a centre-back anymore. There were also questions about his attitude.

'Come on Virgil – *FOCUS!* You look like you're not even trying today.'

It was often his calm playing style that got him into trouble. When Willem were winning a game comfortably, Virgil sometimes switched off and made silly mistakes. But the problem was that even when he was fully focused, he just looked really relaxed.

'I can't help it,' he complained to his teammates after another telling-off from his coach, 'that's just who I am!'

Until then, Virgil had always believed that Willem II would give him his first professional contract.

But now that he was sixteen, that was all in doubt. At that age, the coaches were looking to see who had what it took to become a top professional player, and who didn't. Only the most talented young footballers would make the next step-up to the Willem II Under-19s. And even then, they might not start earning money for another year or two.

So, as Virgil finished high school, he searched for a part-time job that he could fit in around his busy football schedule. Fortunately, he found one, washing dishes at the Oncle Jean restaurant.

'When can you work, kid?' asked the owner, Jacques Lips, when he went along for an interview.

Virgil had checked this carefully. 'Wednesdays and Sundays are the only nights I don't have training or a match.'

'Perfect, those are our busiest times – you've got yourself a job!'

So after day-time practices with Willem II, Virgil would get the train back to Breda station, pick up his bike and cycle fifteen minutes to the restaurant. Then, after finishing his five-hour shift, he would cycle home if he still had any energy left. If not, he would get his dad to come and pick him up.

It wasn't fun, but it was the only way for Virgil to keep his football dream alive. To start with, he didn't say much to anyone at Oncle Jean. He just got on with his boring job in the back of the restaurant.

'You're earning money so that you can go out on Saturday nights with your mates,' he had to keep telling himself during those long, dull hours at the dirty kitchen sink.

But the longer Virgil worked there, the more he got to know his new boss. It turned out that he was a really nice guy and they got on well.

'How would you like to do more shifts and earn some extra money?' Lips suggested one day. 'We need good, hard workers like you.'

'Thanks, but I really don't have time. Sorry, I have to be at the Willem academy every da—'

'I get it – football comes first!' Lips interrupted with a smile. 'That's fine, but are you sure it's worth all this effort? Do you really think you're going to be a professional player one day?'

Virgil nodded confidently. 'Yes, I do. I'm going to be a star!'

'Okay, well if you change your mind and want to earn some extra money, just let me know. Good luck, kid, I hope you make it!'

Virgil really hoped so too. He couldn't give up now, not when he had worked so hard to get this far. And not when the Willem II first team was in sight, training only metres away from them.

'Look, there's Jens Janse. He's a defender like me and he's only twenty-one!'

Virgil was determined to achieve his football dream, but for that to happen, something significant had to change. Thankfully, it soon would.

CHAPTER 7

ONWARDS AND UPWARDS

'Oh my, where has my cute little boy gone?' Hellen teased Virgil as he sat down for breakfast. Suddenly, her eldest son was starting to tower over her.

'I swear you're getting taller and taller every day!'

His mum was right about that. In 2008, Virgil finally had his growth spurt, and it went on and on all summer. He shot up from a pretty average five-foot nine to a gigantic six-foot four.

'You could be a basketball player now!' suggested his brother, who was back to being the smaller one again.

Virgil smiled but shook his head. 'No, I can be a big, powerful centre-back now!'

Hopefully, his days as a right-back were over. He was ready to become the deadliest defender in the world.

When Virgil returned to Willem II for preseason training, the staff just stood there staring at him in shock. Was this really the same kid they had been coaching for years? And Virgil's teammates were just as surprised.

'Woah mate, what happened to you this summer?'

'Watch out, giant coming through!'

'Hey, what's the weather like up there?'

Virgil was delighted with his new-found height, but his body didn't cope well with the changes. At first, he found playing football really painful. Running, kicking, tackling – nothing felt right anymore. It was like he was playing in someone else's body. He had problems with his knees, his hamstrings, his ankles...

Argghhhhh!

'Don't worry, these things are normal at your age,' the coaches reassured him. 'Soon, you'll be better than ever!'

Soon? That was no good – Virgil needed to be better than ever now! Otherwise, he would never move up from the Willem Under-17s to the Under-19s. It was so frustrating for him, but in the end, the only answer was to stop playing and listen to the physio's advice:

'You need to rest and then recover. If you don't, you'll do yourself some serious damage.'

Over the next six weeks, Virgil had to show all of his patience and dedication. He spent hours in the gym, doing the same exercises over and again. It was slow progress, but eventually his body started to feel right again.

'At last!' Virgil cheered with relief. He was finally pain-free, and ready to return to action.

When he made his big comeback, Virgil really was better than ever. The Willem coaches had been right about that. He was still the same calm defender with excellent decision-making skills, but now he had that extra height for winning headers. And an extra burst of speed too, thanks to the physio.

What a complete package! No-one was getting past him now.

An attacker raced down the right wing and tried to pull the ball back to his partner in the middle. Virgil saw it coming and calmly stepped in to deal with the danger. *INTERCEPTION!*

A forward twisted and turned on the edge of the box, looking for a way through. In desperation, he decided to go for goal. It was a decent shot, but Virgil bravely got his big body in the way. *BLOCK!*

A speedy striker chased after a long pass over the top. Although he had a head-start, Virgil got back, and he got the ball too. *RECOVERY!*

A skilful playmaker dribbled his way through the Willem defence. Finally, he was one on one with Virgil, who waited and waited until he was ready to pounce. *TACKLE!*

Their opponents curled a corner into the crowded penalty box, and up jumped Virgil, head and shoulders above the rest. *HEADER!*

With this new and improved version of Virgil in defence, the Willem Under-17s picked up clean sheet after clean sheet. It wasn't long before his performances attracted attention from the age group above.

'This kid could be the next Jaap Stam!' some people predicted. Stam was a top Dutch defender who had spent a season at Willem in the 1990s before moving on to play for Manchester United, Lazio and AC Milan.

Fortunately, Virgil could handle these new high expectations. Soon after joining the Under-19s, he became their captain. He loved the extra responsibility of the role. He was already a leader on the pitch anyway.

'The armband just makes it more official!' Virgil told himself as he organised and encouraged the teammates around him.

After a frustrating few years, suddenly everything was going right for Virgil again. He was even playing some matches for the Under-23s. And from there, it was only one giant leap to the Willem first team. His football dream was alive and kicking.

CHAPTER 8

GOING TO GRONINGEN

Despite all of Virgil's excellent defending, there were some people at Willem who still weren't convinced. Mostly, it came down to the same old issues: his concentration and his calm playing style.

'At this level, he can make a mistake or two and nothing happens,' the reserve team coach Edwin Hermans argued. 'But if he does that stuff in the Dutch League, he'll get destroyed!'

His assistants agreed. 'It's like he switches off and stops trying sometimes when it looks like the game is won. There's no question that he's got the talent to play for the first team, but the attitude? I just don't know.'

To make matters worse for Virgil, the Willem first team was fighting relegation from the Dutch First Division. In that tricky situation, the manager turned to his most experienced professionals, not 'the next big thing'.

But did Virgil really have that much potential anyway? In the end, the club's conclusion was that he was a good young player but not a stand-out future star. So, should they offer him that first contract he was hoping for?

Hermans said yes, but Willem waited too long. While they were still thinking, another club came along who were much more willing to take a risk on Virgil's rising talent.

Groningen were a team in the northern Netherlands with a great record of developing young players and giving them a chance to shine. Several Dutch national team stars had started their careers at Groningen, including Arjen Robben and legendary centre-back Ronald Koeman.

Koeman's dad, Martin, had played for the club too, and he still worked there as the chief scout.

When his colleague Henk Weldmate recommended
a tall, athletic defender in the Willem reserves, he
went along to take a look for himself.

By half-time, Martin Koeman was both impressed
and confused. Why wasn't this kid already playing
for the first team? He was classy on the ball, brave in
the air, and strong in the tackle. No-one had got past
him at all during that half of the match. What else
did Willem want from a young centre-back?

'Yes, he's still a bit raw, but he could be a real
superstar one day!'

Koeman was even more confused when he found
out that Willem hadn't even offered Virgil a first
team contract yet. What were they waiting for?

'Right, we've got to move fast,' Koeman explained
to the Groningen chairman, 'before they realise their
big mistake!'

But if they really wanted to sign Virgil, they would
need to give the boy from Breda a very good reason
to move 200 miles away from his home:

'We believe in you and we want to help you
become an even better player,' the Groningen team

told him in a meeting with his agent.

Virgil had heard all that before but, unlike Willem, they were offering him a proper professional contract to prove it. This changed everything! His football dream would be safe, at least for the next few years.

'Thanks, but can I have a few days to think about it?' Virgil asked. He had a difficult decision to make, and just like when he was out there playing on the football pitch, he preferred to take his time.

It was only when Willem found out about Groningen's offer that they tried to persuade Virgil to stay. But by then, it was too late. Virgil wanted to be at a football club where he felt wanted and valued. His mind was made up; he was going to Groningen.

CHAPTER 9

LEARNING UNDER LUKKIEN

'This is it – I'm a professional footballer now and I'm on my way to the top!'

That's what Virgil was thinking as he arrived at his new club. So what if Willem hadn't wanted him? He didn't need them; he was going to become a world-class defender anyway. First at Groningen, then after that, who knew? Maybe even at Ronaldinho's Barcelona!

However, Virgil didn't get off to the smooth start that he was expecting at Groningen. He was hoping to go straight into the first team squad, but instead, he found himself training with the Under-23s. And when match day came, he was only one of the substitutes.

'What's going on?' Virgil thought to himself as he sat there sulking in angry silence. 'I didn't travel all that way to waste my time like this!'

At Willem, he was hardly ever on the bench. Even during Virgil's worst spell, when the coaches thought he was too small and slow to be a central defender, they had just moved him across to right-back. He was better than the bench! Had he made a massive mistake by going to Groningen? Should he have stayed at home after all?

Virgil wasn't the type of person who kept quiet when something was troubling him. He believed in speaking his mind. So once the game finished, he went straight up to the Under-23s manager and asked him:

'Why am I not playing?'

'Because you're not ready to play,' Dick Lukkien replied simply.

'Yes, I am!' Virgil protested.

'No, you're not.'

Stubborn Virgil had met his match. Lukkien wasn't backing down. Although the Under-23s manager had been impressed by Virgil's talent in training, he had also noticed something else that wasn't so positive. The defender's body was in a really bad way.

'You need to work on building up your fitness first,' Lukkien explained. 'Otherwise, you're going to get a bad injury. How many matches were you playing per week at Willem?'

Virgil shrugged casually. 'Two, sometimes three when they called me up to the Under-23s...'

'I thought so – that's far too much football for a youngster like you! I know you want to reach the first team as quickly as possible, but you can't rush these things. You'll get there, I promise, but right now you need to be patient.'

On the football field, Virgil could wait ages for the perfect moment to make a tackle. But that was because it was fun. Doing lots of boring fitness work in the gym, on the other hand, was not fun at all.

'Keep going, keep going!' the Groningen coaches encouraged him.

That wasn't easy for Virgil, especially as he was so far away from all his friends and family in Breda.

There was no-one to drive him to training, so he had to cycle everywhere. He was on his own now, which meant growing up fast and doing things that he didn't want to do. But through all the challenging and lonely times, Virgil stayed determined about one thing. No matter what, he was going to make his football dream come true…

'Excellent, Virgil!' Lukkien applauded on the touchline. He was delighted with his defender's progress. He looked so much stronger and sharper now. At last, he was ready to play.

And that was just the start of Virgil's learning under Lukkien. In matches, the manager didn't let his star defender relax for a second.

'Virgil, stay focused!'

'I am!'

'No, you're not!'

Lukkien knew how good Virgil could be, but he still got a bit lazy whenever Groningen were winning comfortably. That had to stop. Losing concentration wasn't acceptable anymore, not even for a moment, not if Virgil wanted to move up to the first team.

By pushing him hard, Lukkien got the best out of his classy centre-back. And it worked. In the final weeks of the 2010/11 season, Virgil was called up to the senior Groningen squad for an away game against ADO Den Haag.

'Congratulations, I told you you'd get there in the end!' Lukkien said with a handshake and a smile.

'Thanks, Coach!' Virgil replied, trying his best not to burst with pride. 'Thanks for everything, for believing in me. I know I haven't always showed it, but I'm really grateful for all your help.'

'You deserve it – you've worked hard for this. Good luck, kid, and remember – STAY FOCUSED!'

CHAPTER 10

GRONINGEN'S EMERGENCY EXTRA STRIKER

So, was Virgil about to make his Dutch league debut at the age of just nineteen? When the manager Pieter Huistra announced the starting line-up, he was there on the list of subs:

48 van Dijk.

Wow, it was really happening! And there was a green-and-white shirt waiting for him, with his name and number on the back. Virgil wanted to take a photo to send to his friends and family, but at the same time, he didn't want to embarrass himself in front of his new teammates. He was sharing a dressing room with experienced professionals now. Forward Dušan Tadić was a Serbian international, while defenders Andreas Granqvist and Fredrik Stenman both played for Sweden.

'Just act cool,' Virgil kept telling himself as the clock ticked down to kick-off.

On this occasion, he didn't mind being on the bench. It gave him time to soak up the atmosphere in the stadium and get a sense of the speed and style of the game. By half-time, however, he was getting restless.

'Bring me on, I'm ready!' Virgil wanted to tell his manager, but for once, he kept his thoughts to himself during the team-talk.

Groningen were drawing at that point, but early in the second half, they took the lead again. 3–2! Brilliant, a win would lift them up to fifth place; they could still qualify for the Europa League! What would Huistra do next – go for another goal or strengthen the defence?

Virgil, of course, was hoping for the second option. With twenty minutes to go, he got the call he was waiting for:

'Get ready, you're coming on!'

Virgil wasn't nervous as he ran onto the field for his Groningen debut, just excited. On the outside, he looked as calm and composed as ever, like it was just another average football match.

'You're gonna be great, kid! Just mark him tightly,' Fredrik called out, pointing to one of the ADO strikers.

No problem! At the centre of the defence, Virgil didn't have that much to do, but the whole time he could hear Lukkien's words playing in his head:

'STAY FOCUSED!'

No, there would be no silly mistakes today. No-one was getting past him. At the final whistle, Groningen were 4–2 winners and Virgil walked off the pitch with his head held high. It was a strong start to his professional football career. Fredrik was the first of many teammates and coaches to come over and congratulate him.

'Well done, mate – you're a star in the making!'

Virgil was delighted with his debut performance, and desperate for more game-time straight away. Two weeks later, he came on for the last fifteen minutes against PSV Eindhoven. This time, though, he was playing in a very different position.

In order to finish fourth and qualify for the Europa League, Groningen had to win. A 0–0 score would not be enough. So Huistra turned to his subs bench, looking for another attacking option. What about Virgil? With his height, strength and skill, the manager decided that he could be an excellent emergency extra striker.

'I want you to go up front and win every header,' his manager explained to him.

Virgil's childhood dream was coming true! He did his best to flick balls on for Dušan and Tim Matavž, but sadly Groningen just could not find that winning goal.

Noooooooooo! Many of the players collapsed to the floor in disappointment, but Virgil stood tall and strong. It wasn't over yet; Groningen could still qualify for the Europa League through the play-offs.

'Come on, we can do this!' Virgil urged his teammates. Even at such a young age, he wasn't shy about speaking up.

Together, they battled their way past Heracles Almelo to set up a final against... ADO Den Haag again! Groningen were feeling confident; too confident, it turned out. In the first leg, they were thrashed 5–1. 5–1! Was that their Europa League dream over?

No way! Virgil still believed. In the second leg at home at the Noordlease Stadium, he started his first ever game for Groningen. Huistra picked him to play at right-back, but before long, he was on the attack again...

Early in the second half, Groningen won a free kick on the left side of the ADO box. Three players – Petter Andersson, Leandro Bacuna and Virgil – stood around the ball, discussing who would take it.

'Trust me, I've got this,' Virgil assured the others.

As well as being a top defender, Virgil was also a free kick king. He could strike the ball with lots of power, swerve and accuracy. BANG! His shot curled around the wall and then dipped down into the bottom corner.

Goooooooooooooaaaaaaaaalllllllllllllllll!!!!!!!!!!!!!!!!!

What a time and what a way for Virgil to score his first Groningen goal! He got hugs and high-fives from his teammates, but they didn't have time to celebrate properly. It was now 3–6 on aggregate – Groningen had forty minutes left to score another three goals at least.

'Come on, we can do this!'

Leandro fired in a long-range rocket. 4–6!

Virgil was now playing as an emergency extra striker again. When Petter dribbled forward, he timed his run perfectly and then, with his weaker left foot, squeezed a shot under the ADO keeper. 5–6!

Gooooooooooooooooooooaaaaaaaaaaaaaaaaallllllllllll llllllllllllll!!!!!!!!!!!!!!!!!!!

Two goals on his full Groningen debut – Virgil was a club hero already!

'Are you sure you're a defender?' Petter joked as they rushed back for the restart.

Virgil smiled and shrugged. 'I can play anywhere!'

Groningen, however, still needed one more goal.

Virgil flicked a header on to Tim, who shot just wide. *CLOSE!*

Tim was through one-on-one with the keeper, but his chip hit the crossbar. *EVEN CLOSER!*

Groningen weren't giving up. In the eighty-ninth minute, Dušan curled one last corner into the ADO box. As the ball bounced down, Tim reacted first. His shot was going in, until it struck a defender on the arm.

'Penalty!' cried Virgil, along with all his teammates and the thousands of supporters in the stadium.

The referee pointed to the spot and Tim stepped up and scored. 6–6!

What an incredible game! Virgil was desperate to keep playing, but he was absolutely exhausted after his goalscoring efforts. As he hobbled off in extra time, the Groningen fans gave him a standing ovation.

Virgil! Virgil! Virgil!

'What a performance, kid!' Huistra said, giving him a great big hug.

Virgil slumped down in his seat on the bench to watch the rest of the drama unfold: twenty tense minutes of football and then a penalty shoot-out.

'I should be out there taking one!' Virgil thought

to himself. He loved the pressure, and he could strike a penalty just as well as he could strike a free kick, if not better.

But there was nothing Virgil could do now, except hope and cheer. He could feel his heart pounding in his chest as one by one his teammates stepped up to take a spot-kick.

'Go on, Andreas!'

'Yes, Thomas!'

'Nice one, Dušan!'

After nine penalties, ADO were 4–3 up. It was all up to Tim now – could he score from the spot again?

'Come on, come on,' Virgil muttered under his breath.

The keeper dived the wrong way, but Tim's powerful shot smacked against the crossbar.

Nooooooooooo! Again, the Groningen players collapsed to the floor in disappointment. This time, their Europa League dream really was over.

Virgil felt their pain and frustration, but he also felt a lot of pride too. His football career had come a long way in such short period of time. Only a month before, he had been training with the Under-23s, and learning under Lukkien. Now, Virgil was a first team regular, a classy young defender, a free kick king, a club hero and Groningen's emergency extra striker.

CHAPTER 11

A HORRIBLE TIME
IN HOSPITAL

Soon after the 2011/12 season kicked off, Virgil's
days as Groningen's emergency extra striker came
to an end. That's because he was now the club's
first-choice centre-back. With Andreas and Fredrik
both gone, he was the new leader in defence.

Virgil loved the responsibility of the role. Out
on the football field, he was always talking, always
organising his teammates:

'Kees, that's your man!'

'Tim, drop deeper!'

'Johan, get tighter!'

Virgil still made a few silly mistakes now and then
when he got too comfortable, but when he stayed

fully focused and read the game well, no-one could get past him. And it was in the biggest games that Virgil shone the brightest. With him at the heart of their defence, Groningen beat Ajax 1–0 and then Feyenoord 6–0.

That day, Virgil was head and shoulders above everyone else. In the very first minute, he intercepted a through-ball and then launched a beautiful long pass from right to left to set Dušan away and score. *1–0!*

'What a ball!' his goalscoring teammate thanked him with a double-five.

Eighty-eight impressive minutes later, Virgil made it 5–0 with an unbelievable shot from nearly forty yards. As the ball flew past him, the Feyenoord goalkeeper just sat down and gave up. He had no chance of stopping a thunderstrike like that.

Goooooooooooooooooooooaaaaaaaaaaaaaaaaallllllllllll llllllllllllll!!!!!!!!!!!!!!!!!!

'Mate, you're amazing!' Leandro cheered, leaping into his tall teammate's arms.

Virgil stood there smiling and beating his chest

with pride. Not bad for his first goal in the Dutch league! He would never forget his man-of-the-match performance, and neither would the Feyenoord manager, Ronald Koeman.

'My dad was right about that big Groningen centre-back,' Koeman muttered to himself. 'If he keeps improving, he could be the next superstar Dutch defender.'

But just when everything seemed to be going so well for Virgil, disaster struck. It all started with a bad stomach ache in the days before the big local derby against Heerenveen.

'It's a sign that you need to start eating more healthily,' the club doctor Henk Hagenauw warned him. 'When was the last time you had a proper meal?'

Virgil shrugged. He was living with his young teammate, Tim Keurntjes, and neither of them had a clue about cooking. 'Does McDonald's count?' he asked, knowing the answer.

Hagenauw rolled his eyes. 'I'm serious – you can't keep filling your body with junk food all the time. You're a professional footballer now and diet is really important. Look, eat lots of fruit and vegetables and see if it gets any better.'

But a few days passed, and Virgil's pain grew worse. Would he have to miss the big derby match? It got so bad that in the end, he had to wake Tim up in the middle of the night and ask him to drive him to the hospital.

'Arggghhhh!' Virgil screamed out in agony. 'Are we there yet? How much further?'

When he got to the hospital, the news wasn't good. Virgil had ruptured his appendix and that was just one of many medical problems.

'You're lucky to be alive,' the doctors told him, 'and you're going to need major surgery.'

Major surgery? Virgil couldn't believe it. It was the first day of April – April Fool's Day – but this was no time for joking, no laughing matter. This was serious.

Like most twenty-year-olds, Virgil had thought that he was invincible. Until now. Now, he was lying in a hospital bed, unable to do anything, and his body was in a really bad way. Now, he wasn't just fighting for his football career; he was also fighting for his life.

'How are you feeling?' his mum asked anxiously from the chair next to his bed. As soon as she got the phone call, Hellen had rushed up from Breda to be by his side. She couldn't let her eldest son go through this alone.

'Not great,' Virgil replied honestly.

For two long, slow, boring weeks, that hospital became his home. During much of that time, Virgil couldn't do anything except sit, sleep, rest and pray that he would get better. But slowly, after days of rest, his body grew stronger and stronger, until eventually he was able to walk again. Those first steps were so tiring, but Virgil was determined to get back on his feet and back out on the pitch as soon as possible.

'So, when can I start playing football again?' he asked, crossing all his fingers and toes.

'Virgil!' Hellen said, sighing loudly. How could he even think about that yet, when he had only just had major surgery?

'Your mum's right – I'm afraid that football will have to wait,' the doctor explained. 'Remember, you've lost a lot of weight and strength. It'll take time to build you back up. But if everything goes well with your recovery, you could be back fit for next season.'

'Next season' – it wasn't the answer that Virgil had been hoping for, but it was still a whole lot better than 'Never'. In fact, it was only a few months away. Yet again in his football career, he would just have to be patient and work hard. But after his horrible time in hospital, Virgil didn't mind so much. He felt lucky to be alive at all.

Those two weeks were the wake-up call that Virgil needed. From now on, he decided, he was going to be a disciplined, dedicated professional. He would take good care of his body and eat a balanced, healthy diet.

No, Virgil wasn't going to let anything like that get in the way of his football dream again.

CHAPTER 12

SAYING YES TO CELTIC

After his horrible time in hospital, Virgil came back stronger, faster, more determined and more unbeatable than ever. Groningen's new Number 6 only missed two league matches during the whole 2012/13 season, and that was only because of suspension.

With their best defender back, Groningen became much harder to beat. They finished the season in seventh place, just missing out on the Europa League again.

So close! Sadly, Virgil knew that was probably as good as it would ever get for him at Groningen. Most talented players at mid-table Dutch clubs eventually moved up to one of the country's top three teams: Ajax, Feyenoord or PSV Eindhoven.

'I'm ready for that next step now,' Virgil told his agent confidently.

During the summer of 2013, two of those top clubs were looking to sign new young centre-backs: Ajax and PSV. And there were three names at the top of both of their lists:

Mike van der Hoorn from FC Utrecht,

Jeffrey Bruma from Chelsea,

and Virgil van Dijk from Groningen.

So which one would they choose? Virgil had a positive meeting with Ajax's Director of Football, Marc Overmars, but in the end, the club signed van der Hoorn instead. PSV, meanwhile, went for Bruma, and Feyenoord stuck with Stefan de Vrij and Bruno Martins Indi.

What about Virgil? Well, he had nowhere left to go in the Netherlands.

'Why don't they want me?' he asked himself. Virgil thought back to his performances against the top teams that season. Yes, he had made a few silly mistakes, but nothing too serious. And for every error, there were loads of examples of excellent defending…

Or perhaps it was the same old issue: Virgil's casual playing style. He wasn't a typical big, brave centre-back who threw himself into every tackle. Instead, he read the game well and got into the right positions to win the ball in other ways. Did the top Dutch clubs really think that he didn't care when he was on the football pitch?

'Forget about it,' his agent told him, 'there are plenty of other clubs in other countries.'

What about Brighton, who had just missed out on promotion to the English Premier League?

'No, I want to play in one of the top leagues in Europe,' Virgil decided.

What about FC Krasnodar, a Russian team who were offering Virgil a big money move?

'No, I want to play in one of the top leagues in Europe.'

What about Celtic, the Champions of Scotland?

'You'd get the chance to play in the Champions League,' his agent added as an extra fact to tempt him.

It worked – that was Virgil's football dream. If
there was the chance to play in Europe's greatest
club competition, then he was in!

'And they really want to sign me?' he asked
his agent.

Yes! Having sold Kelvin Wilson to Nottingham
Forest, Celtic needed a new star centre-back. After
months of searching, their chief scout, John Park,
handed a shortlist to the manager, Neil Lennon.
There were two names at the top:

Mike van der Hoorn from FC Utrecht.

Virgil van Dijk from Groningen.

They were both brilliant defenders, but Park
preferred Virgil. He had the confidence to try things
that others didn't, especially when he brought the
ball out from the back. He was different, special.

'Right, well I better go and take a look at him in
action then,' Lennon declared.

By half-time, the Celtic manager was both
impressed and confused. Why wasn't Virgil already
playing for one of the top clubs in Europe? He had
amazing composure, strength, speed and technique.

What else could you want from a young centre-back?

'Wow, this guy's got everything!' he thought to himself.

And best of all, Virgil was available to buy for less than £3 million. What a bargain! Lennon couldn't believe his luck – what were Celtic waiting for?

'Right, we've got to move fast,' he explained to the chairman, 'before the big Premier League clubs come looking at him!'

When he met with Celtic, Virgil was impressed immediately. It was a famous club with an incredible history. The chance to play in the Champions League was a key factor, of course, but most of all, he just wanted to be at a football club where he felt wanted and valued. That's why he had gone from Willem II to Groningen, and that's why he said yes to Celtic.

'It feels very good and I'm very excited to be here,' Virgil told the Scottish media as he held up a green-and-white hooped shirt with the Number 5 on the back.

The Celtic manager was very excited too, and soon, so were the players. The first thing they noticed about Virgil was his size. At six-foot four, he looked like a basketball player, but once the training session started, it was clear that Virgil was a football superstar. The club's strikers all lined up to test their new Dutch defender: Georgios Samaras, Teemu Pukki, Kris Commons, Anthony Stokes, Leigh Griffiths… But as hard as they tried, no-one could get past him.

'What is this guy doing here?' his new teammates wondered. 'He should be playing for Real Madrid or Manchester United, not Celtic!'

And no-one could get the ball off him either. Wouldn't he be wasted in defence? With his touch and technique, Virgil could easily move into midfield instead. Whatever position he played, Celtic would need to make the most of his time at the club.

'Enjoy yourself,' Lennon told his new star signing. 'I've got a feeling that you won't be here for long!'

CHAPTER 13

A STRONG START IN SCOTLAND

Virgil's first year at Celtic was an all-round success. Not only did he become the club's rock at the back, but he also showed his quality in attack.

Before all that, however, Virgil needed a bit of time to get used to life in Scotland. He had to adapt to a new country, a new league, the sometimes dreary weather and the always difficult accent. When he first arrived, he thought that he spoke English pretty well. But when his Scottish teammates started talking, he found that he could hardly understand a word!

'Could you say that again,' Virgil asked politely at first, 'and a little more slowly this time?'

But when he still didn't understand, he decided it was easier to just nod instead.

On the pitch, Virgil settled in quickly at Celtic. His class was clear right from his debut – a 2–0 win against Aberdeen – but he had to wait three long months to score his first goal for his new club. Finally, away at Ross County, he went forward for a free kick and jumped the highest to meet Emilio Izaguirre's cross. His header bounced down, hit the post and then the back of the net.

Gooooooooooooooooooooaaaaaaaaaaaaaaaaalllllllllllll llllllllllllll!!!!!!!!!!!!!!!!!!!!!!

There was no big celebration from Virgil, just a casual jog towards the Celtic fans near the corner flag. He was a cool guy, after all.

'At last, big man!' his captain Scott Brown cried out.

Virgil only had to wait another twelve minutes to score his second Celtic goal. As Charlie Mulgrew curled a corner into the box, he made a late sprint from the edge of the area to the six-yard box and flicked the ball down into the bottom corner. He was a brilliant attacking defender, especially for a centre-back. *2–0!* On the touchline, Lennon clapped and smiled. What a signing!

Now that Virgil was off the mark, there was no stopping him. Against St. Johnstone, he got the ball in his own half and dribbled forward, through one tackle, then another, then another. What a run! He made it look so easy. He was into the penalty area now, and he calmly poked the ball past the keeper.

Goooooooooooooooooooooaaaaaaaaaaaaaaaaaallllllllllll llllllllllllllll!!!!!!!!!!!!!!!!!!!!!

It was a wondergoal, the best that Virgil had scored since his days on the Cruyff court in Breda. Even Ronaldinho or Messi would have been proud of a solo run like that. As he ran past the celebrating Celtic fans, Virgil made a heart symbol with his hands. He was having so much fun playing for this football club.

'Put van Dijk up front!' many of the supporters suggested after that.

But if they did that, Celtic would lose their best centre-back! When he played in defence, Virgil could star at both ends of the field. Against Hibernian, he kept the strikers quiet and then fired an unstoppable free kick into the top corner. The shot was so good that Lennon got up off the bench to give him a standing ovation.

'Is there anything this guy can't do?' his manager wondered to himself.

Celtic still hadn't lost a single league match all season. And as the games went by, they became even harder to beat. Virgil formed a formidable centre-back partnership with Efe Ambrose, a powerful defender from Nigeria. Once they got used to playing together, no-one could get past them. And if they ever did, they had keeper Fraser Forster to beat. From December until late February, Celtic's defence didn't concede a single goal. The clean sheets just kept coming and coming:

5–0, 1–0, 2–0, 1–0, 1–0, 1–0, 4–0, 3–0...

After an amazing 1,256 minutes of Scottish Premier League football, Celtic finally let a goal in against Aberdeen, but that was only because Virgil had been sent off for a late, last-ditch tackle.

'Sorry, guys, I let you down there,' he apologised

to his fellow defenders in the dressing room afterwards. Although they had set a new club record together, he still felt bad about bringing their brilliant run to an end.

'Hey, just don't do it again, okay?' Fraser said with a reassuring smile. 'We need you out there on the pitch!'

It was true; what would Celtic do without their star centre-back? Virgil returned from suspension just in time for their trip to Partick Thistle in late March 2014. With a victory, they would be crowned the Champions of Scotland again, with a whopping seven games to spare. The title hadn't been won that early since 1929.

'Come on, let's do this!' Scott roared as the players left the dressing room.

Virgil couldn't wait to win his first major trophy as a professional footballer. He had waited a long time for this moment. In the fourth minute, he passed the ball forward to Kris Commons, who played it out wide to Emilio, who crossed it into Anthony Stokes. *1–0!*

By the end of the game, it was 5–1 to Celtic, the perfect way to win their third title in a row. At the final whistle, Virgil and his teammates hugged and celebrated their success. Yes, glory was expected when you played for a top team in Scotland, but they had worked really hard all season long to reach their target.

When the players returned to the dressing room, Virgil was one of the first to put on a special green T-shirt with '14 CHAMPIONS' written on the back. He wrapped a Celtic scarf around his neck, and jumped up on the benches to sing along with all the others:

Campeones, Campeones, Olé! Olé! Olé!

For the proper trophy presentation, however, Virgil had to wait until after Celtic's final league game of the season, at home against Dundee United. Following a comfortable 3–1 victory, the pitch was cleared, and a green-and-white stage was set up in the centre circle.

Then one by one, the players walked up to collect their winners' medals. When it was Virgil's turn, he waved to the supporters and to his family and friends in the crowd. It was lovely to share this special day with them all.

At last, it was time for the main event.

'10, 9, 8, 7…,' the Celtic fans counted down, '…3, 2, 1… HURRAAAAAAAYYY!'

As Scott lifted the SPFL trophy high into the sky, Virgil was right behind him with his arms up in the air. Winning was simply the greatest feeling in the world.

Virgil had really enjoyed his first season at Celtic. Not only had he lifted the league title, but he had also been selected for the Scottish Team of the Year and named on the shortlist for the Player of the Year award. All at the age of only twenty-one.

Hopefully, there would be plenty more success to come. Although it sometimes looked like it was all too easy for him, Virgil was still learning lots. And best of all, he was gaining valuable European experience.

CHAPTER 14

EUROPEAN EXPERIENCE

With a cheeky nutmeg, Andrés Iniesta escaped past Efe and into the Celtic six-yard box. 'Uh-oh,' the fans thought, but out of nowhere, another defender slid across to make the saving tackle. Who was it? Virgil, of course!

Celtic Park let out an almighty roar. The atmosphere in the stadium was always great, but on big European nights like this one in October 2013, it was electric. Thanks to their top Dutch defender, they were still drawing 0–0 with Barcelona.

Come on, Celtic!

Virgil felt another rush of adrenaline flow through his body. This was what playing professional football was all about – the crowds, the competition, the pressure to perform. He was born to play on the biggest stage.

The Champions League was proving to be just the challenge that Virgil needed. Despite a strong performance against AC Milan at the San Siro, Celtic had conceded two cruel, late goals. Arghhhhh! That was a painful learning experience for all of them.

But now, they had the chance to bounce back against Barcelona. Although Messi was missing through injury, the Spanish side still had Iniesta, Neymar Jr, Cesc Fàbregas and Pedro, plus Alexis Sánchez on the bench.

Not one of them could get past Virgil, though. He was having one of his greatest games in a Celtic shirt. He had too much speed and strength for the Barcelona forwards, and he always seemed to know what they would do next. He won every header and intercepted every through-ball.

From start to finish, the Celtic fans cheered their beloved defender on.

Olé, Olé, Olé, Olé, Virgil van Dijk, Dijk!

With him at the back, they believed they could beat any team in the world.

Celtic looked pretty comfortable for the first sixty minutes, but then Scott got sent off. Suddenly, that changed everything. Could they really hold on against Barcelona, with only ten men? Virgil did his best. He blocked shots from Xavi, then Pedro, and then Neymar Jr.

Olé, Olé, Olé, Olé, Virgil van Dijk, Dijk!

But the Barcelona attacks kept coming. In the seventy-fifth minute, Sánchez got the ball out wide on the right wing and crossed it into the box. The Celtic defence thought they had it covered, but no, somehow Fàbregas had a free header at the back post. 1–0!

As the ball landed in the back of the net, Virgil turned away in anger. For once, he was lost for words on the football pitch. Who was meant to be marking Fàbregas, and why had they let him escape? One mistake and all their hard work was wasted!

It was another painful Champions League learning experience for Celtic, and there were more to come.

In the away game at the Nou Camp two months later, Barcelona thrashed them 6–1, even without Messi. And it could have been even worse if it wasn't for Virgil.

Against the best attackers in the world, the Dutch defender raised his game to the highest level. Neymar Jr dribbled forward, with Xavi to his right. It was two against one, but Virgil waited for the Brazilian to make his move. On the edge of the Celtic penalty area, Neymar Jr played the pass, but Virgil read the situation superbly. In a flash, he turned and stretched out a leg to beat Xavi to the ball.

'Yes, that's it!' the Celtic supporters cheered.

Again and again, Virgil dealt with the Barcelona danger. But he couldn't do it all on his own.

'Come on, help me out here!' he screamed at his struggling teammates, as yet another goal went in.

Even in a 6–1 defeat, Virgil put on a one-man defensive masterclass. He didn't deserve to be on the losing team, and he definitely didn't deserve to score an own goal. But football could be a cruel game sometimes. Virgil had learnt that a long time ago. And if he wanted to be the best, he had to battle against the best. As frustrating as it felt, it was all good European experience for him.

'You were magnificent tonight,' Virgil's manager told him after the match. 'You should be really proud of that performance.'

Unfortunately, that was the end of Celtic's Champions League adventure. The next season, they entered the Europa League instead. Virgil and his teammates still got to play against quality opponents, though. After getting through the group stage, they travelled to the San Siro Stadium again, this time to take on Inter Milan.

Could Virgil put on another excellent European performance? He was up against Mauro Icardi, one of the top young strikers in the world.

'Let the battle begin!' Virgil thought to himself.

He was usually so composed in defence, but for once, he lost his cool.

In the twenty-seventh minute, Virgil rushed into a challenge on Inter's second striker, Rodrigo Palacio, and fouled him from behind. The referee blew his whistle – free kick and a yellow card!

Although Virgil thought a booking was a bit harsh, he didn't argue. He just got on with the game, knowing that he had to be more careful now...

But in the thirty-sixth minute, Icardi got to the ball first and flicked it on. As Virgil tried to outmuscle him, he tripped the Inter striker, who fell to the floor. The referee blew his whistle again – another free kick and another yellow card!

As the official reached for the red card in his pocket, Virgil shook his head in disbelief. 'No way, you can't send me off for that!'

But he could and he did. Celtic battled on without their star centre-back, but it was no use, and Inter scored a late winner to knock them out of the Europa League. As the goal went in, Virgil's shoulders slumped.

'It's all my fault,' he thought to himself. 'Why didn't I wait like I usually do? Only fools rush in!'

Oh well – it was another European experience for Virgil to learn from.

CHAPTER 15

SIGNING FOR SOUTHAMPTON

As Virgil relaxed in the sun on his summer holidays, he thought again about his footballing future. He had just turned twenty-four, which felt like an important age. He was no longer a promising young player; he was now in his prime. So, was it time to move on and test himself in one of Europe's top leagues?

'With your talent, you could go anywhere you want!' his friends and family reminded him.

Virgil had really enjoyed his two seasons at Celtic. He had won his first professional trophies there: two Scottish League titles and a League Cup too. He had scored his best ever goal and played some of his greatest games, especially in Europe.

Virgil loved the club dearly: the coaches, the players and, of course, the fantastic fans. It really felt like one big family. Celtic were the team who had taken a chance on him when others wouldn't, and he was so grateful for that. He had learned so much, in the Champions League in particular.

'But now I want to play in the Premier League,' Virgil admitted to his best friends at the club.

They all understood. As Lennon had said to him when he first arrived from Groningen, no-one expected a superstar like Virgil to stay at Celtic for long.

'Well, let's wait and see whether we make it to the Champions League Group Stage,' he decided eventually.

In the qualifying rounds, Celtic stormed past Stjarnan from Iceland and then squeezed past Qarabağ from Azerbaijan.

'Yeess!' Virgil shouted, pumping his fists at the fans. After another strong defensive display, they had secured a win *and* a clean sheet.

Celtic were now just one round away from reaching the Champions League group stage.

The last team standing in their way were Malmö. Celtic won the first leg 3–2 at home at Celtic Park, but in the second leg in Sweden, they threw it away.

'Nooo!' Virgil groaned, swiping angrily at the air. 'Come on, we're better than that!'

Sadly, Celtic would be playing in the Europa League instead. But would their star centre-back still be there? It looked very unlikely because Virgil had received an interesting offer from England.

Southampton weren't in the Champions League, or the Europa League, but they were doing well in the Premier League. The Saints had finished eighth and then seventh in the last two seasons. And their manager? The ex-Feyenoord manager and Dutch defensive legend, Ronald Koeman, who was also the son of Martin, the man who had first scouted Virgil at Groningen!

It was simply meant to be. Southampton needed a new defender because their Belgian centre-back Toby Alderweireld had moved to Tottenham. And when the club scouts showed him their shortlist, Koeman knew instantly which one he wanted: Virgil!

The Saints manager thought back to that awful day when Groningen thrashed his Feyenoord side 6–1. Despite the team's attacking quality, it was their tall, classy centre-back who had been the standout player.

'If he keeps improving,' Koeman had said to himself, 'he could be the next superstar Dutch defender.'

Well now, three years later, it was time for Koeman to help turn Virgil into a Premier League superstar. In early September 2015, Celtic accepted Southampton's offer of £13 million. That was a lot of money for a player arriving from Scotland, but it was worth it, the Saints were sure.

'This is the perfect step for me right now,' Virgil told the journalists when his transfer was announced. He knew all about the club's reputation for developing top young players – Gareth Bale, Theo Walcott, Adam Lallana, Luke Shaw. Hopefully, he would be next. 'I just want to play as much as possible and show everyone what I'm capable of.'

Although the season had already started, Virgil was able to settle in quickly at Southampton, just like he had at Celtic. It helped that he had a Dutch manager and some Dutch teammates too.

'Welkom!' said midfielder Jordy Clasie, who had arrived from Feyenoord.

'Hallo!' said defender Cuco Martina, who had arrived from FC Twente.

Plus, there was also a familiar face from Virgil's Groningen days.

'Dušan!' he shouted, giving his old friend a big hug.

It also helped that Virgil was a confident character and a very talented footballer. Yes, he was the new kid at the club, but that didn't mean he was going to keep quiet and show too much respect to his new teammates. He wanted to impress everyone with his all-round game: his strength, speed, skill and positioning. It didn't take long. By the end of his first training session, the Southampton players were delighted with their new signing.

'I'm so glad he's on our team,' the Saints attackers said to each other. 'It must be horrible playing against him in a real match!'

Salomón Rondón and Rickie Lambert found that out for themselves when Virgil made his

Southampton debut against West Brom. As hard as
the strikers tried, they couldn't find a way past him,
and the game finished 0–0. Virgil was delighted
to get a clean sheet straight away. He had passed
his first Premier League test with top marks. He
felt comfortable already, as if he had been playing
alongside José Fonte for years.

'What a start!' his centre-back partner cheered as
they high-fived.

And two weeks later, Virgil gave the Saints fans
even more to cheer about. At home at the St Mary's
Stadium, he went forward for an early corner against
Swansea City. As James Ward-Prowse's cross came
in, Virgil made his move towards the front post.
Then he leapt up and guided a header down into
the bottom corner. He was so good at that attacking
header. *1–0!*

*Goooooooooooooooooooooaaaaaaaaaaaaaaaaalllllllllllll
lllllllllllllll!!!!!!!!!!!!!!!!!!!!*

Virgil had his first Premier League goal! He ran
over to the Saints fans behind the goal with his arms
out wide – he was becoming a club hero already!

Usually he was so calm and composed out on the football pitch, but this was a very special moment. By the corner flag, Virgil jumped up and punched the air with passion.

'Come on!'

In the second half, Dušan made it 2–0 and Sadio Mané made it 3–0. Southampton were flying, just like their new star centre-back.

CHAPTER 16

DUTCH DEBUT
AT LAST!

In the autumn of 2015, a few weeks after his move to Southampton, Virgil finally got the phone call that he had been waiting years for – he had been selected to play for the Netherlands national team!

'Thank you very much, it's a real honour,' he told the new coach, Danny Blind, trying to sound as calm and polite as possible.

As soon as the call was over, however, Virgil danced around the room, yelling at the top of his voice. 'I'm going to be an international!'

It was his childhood dream come true. Although he was very proud of having family from Suriname, he had always wanted to play football for the

Netherlands. It was his home, the country where he had lived for most of his life. He couldn't wait to pull on the famous orange shirt again, and this time, for the senior team.

Back in 2011, when he was first starting out at Groningen, Virgil had played for the Netherlands Under-19s and then the Under-21s. His international career had been going well, until one terrible game against Italy.

That day, Lorenzo Insigne and Ciro Immobile destroyed the young Dutch defence. The humiliating defeat was far from just Virgil's fault, but he did miss a few crucial tackles. And so when the next Netherlands Under-21 squad was picked, his name wasn't there.

'Never mind,' Virgil thought, trying to stay positive. He would just focus on his club football instead.

Three years later, there had been talk of a call-up to the Netherlands senior squad for the 2014 World Cup. At that time, Virgil was playing well at Celtic and the national coach, Louis van Gaal, needed new defenders.

'Take a look at van Dijk,' his coaches suggested. 'The kid's got real quality.'

But in the end, van Gaal decided that starring in the Scottish League didn't mean that Virgil was good enough to go to the World Cup. He picked Terence Kongolo and Bruno Martins Indi instead.

'Never mind,' Virgil thought, trying to stay positive. It hurt, but he believed that if he kept focusing on his club football, one day his international call-up would come.

And now, at last, in October 2015, it had arrived. He was going to make his Dutch debut! For the first time in ages, Virgil was a little nervous as he joined up with the squad for the UEFA Euro 2016 qualifier against Kazakhstan. Would the senior players like Robin van Persie and Wesley Sneijder welcome him into the team?

Virgil didn't need to be nervous, though. He was one of many new, young players in the squad, and he was already friends with Gini Wijnaldum and Daley Blind from the Under-21s. They were all part of the Netherlands' exciting next generation.

'Let's show we're ready to shine!' the young
Dutch stars declared.

Virgil started at centre-back alongside Jeffrey
Bruma, the defender that PSV had chosen to sign
instead of him. There were no hard feelings, though;
they were national teammates now and they had to
work together.

'That's your man, Jeff!'

'Step up, Virg!'

For the first ninety minutes, however, they didn't
have much to do in defence. Georginio scored the first
goal and Wesley scored the second. The Netherlands
were cruising to a comfortable victory on Virgil's debut.

But comfortable could be dangerous for Virgil.
That's when his concentration slipped, and he made
silly mistakes. Sadly, he didn't have his old coach
Liekken's words playing in his head:

'STAY FOCUSED!'

In the last minute, a cross came in and Virgil got
caught in the middle between the two Kazakhstan
strikers. One headed the ball across to the other.
GOAL!

'Noooooo!' Virgil shouted, kicking the air in frustration. It was not the way that he wanted his first game to end. That was the end of their clean sheet, but at least he still had a victory on his Dutch debut.

Three days later, Virgil's second cap ended in a disappointing defeat. At half-time against the Czech Republic, the Netherlands were already 2–0 down.

For the first goal, Virgil got dragged out of defence and dived into a tackle. He didn't get the ball and he couldn't get back in time to stop Pavel Kadeřábek from scoring either.

'Why did I do that?' Virgil screamed up at the sky. He was usually so cool and composed.

That mistake was still on his mind ten minutes later, when Josef Šural dribbled into the box. This time, Virgil didn't dive in. He waited, blocking the passing option, but the Czech forward dribbled past him easily instead and scored.

Oh dear, what a disaster! This time, Virgil kept his eyes fixed down at his feet. He was furious with himself and he couldn't bear to see the looks that the other Netherlands players were giving him. It was such a horrible feeling to know that he was the one to blame.

'Hey, these things happen,' his manager tried to comfort him at half-time. 'Don't worry about it, just learn from it.'

In the second half, however, Blind decided to take Virgil off and bring on a striker. The Netherlands fought back after that, but they still lost 3–2.

Uh oh, was Virgil's international career about to end before it had even started? No, he was a confident character; he could come back from this. The Dutch team was going through a difficult time and he was determined to play an important part in turning things around. With the team failing to qualify for Euro 2016, its coaches were looking to the future.

CHAPTER 17

SHINING AT SOUTHAMPTON

Back in the Premier League, Virgil was doing a great job at Southampton of stopping the top strikers from scoring. At first, he watched videos to work out their weaknesses, but mostly, he just focused on using all of his own strengths.

He outmuscled Arsenal's Olivier Giroud,

He outran Everton's Romelu Lukaku,

He stuck tight to Tottenham's Harry Kane,

And he read the clever moves that Manchester United's Wayne Rooney tried to make.

Then once he had the ball, Virgil coolly dribbled forward or passed it to a teammate. Everything he did looked so effortless and classy, even the tough tackles.

'We love you, Virgil!' the Saints supporters
cheered. The Dutch defender had to be one of their
best signings ever.

Virgil's calm confidence was rubbing off on the
rest of the Southampton team. From January 2016
onwards, they won twelve of their last eighteen
league games, against the likes of Manchester United,
Manchester City, Tottenham – *and* Liverpool.

'Come on you Saints!' Virgil cheered crazily when
Sadio scored the winning goal against The Reds at St
Mary's. From 2–0 down, they had fought their way
back to a famous 3–2 victory.

Southampton now had a strong team spirit and
big game players at both ends of the pitch – Sadio in
attack and Virgil at the back. Together, they led their
team up the table and all the way to sixth place. It
was Southampton's best league finish since 1985.

For Virgil, it was the best possible start to life in
the Premier League. Some critics had suggested that
the step-up from Celtic would be too big for him,
but he had proved them all wrong. At the club's
end of season awards ceremony, he was voted the

Players' Player of the Year and the Fans' Player of the Year.

As Virgil made his way up to the stage, wearing a smart black suit and tie, the whole room began to sing:

We've got Van Dijk,
Virgil Van Dijk,
I just don't think you understand,
He's Ronald Koeman's man,
He's better than Zidane,
We've got Virgil van Dijk!!

Wow, what was he supposed to say after an amazing welcome like that? At first, all he could do was laugh and smile. He was used to hearing his song in the stadium, but not at a fancy awards ceremony!

'I want to thank everyone who voted for me,' Virgil managed to say eventually. 'I'm lost for words – I'm just very happy!'

Virgil couldn't wait for his second Premier League

season to start, but meanwhile, in the summer of 2016, Southampton said goodbye to their manager, Koeman, and more of their best players. Graziano Pellè went to China, Victor Wanyama went to Tottenham, and even Virgil's friend Sadio went to Liverpool.

'No, not you too!' Virgil joked, but really, he was happy for his friend.

Sadio smiled, 'Hey, you'll be joining me there soon – I'm sure of it!'

That sounded awesome, but to make his dream move happen, Virgil needed to keep shining at Southampton a little longer. Once again, he set about stopping the top strikers in the Premier League: Leicester City's Jamie Vardy, Manchester City's Sergio Agüero, and now Liverpool's Sadio Mané.

'Man, I hate playing against you!' his friend complained as they hugged after a hard-fought 0–0 draw at St Mary's. 'It's like you can read my mind every time!'

Virgil laughed. 'That's a shame, mate, because I love playing against you!'

And thanks to their sixth-place finish, Southampton were also through to the Europa League group stage. There, they would face Sparta Prague, Hapoel Be'er Sheva, and Virgil's old enemy, Inter Milan.

Yes, it was time for his rematch with Mauro Icardi, Inter's ace Argentinian striker. Virgil had lost their last battle by getting sent off before half-time.

'Not this time,' he told himself. 'I'm ready to get my revenge!'

However, Inter won 1–0 at the San Siro and they went 1–0 up at St Mary's too, thanks to a goal from Icardi.

'Noooooooo!' Virgil groaned, swiping the air angrily. He had been too busy stopping Inter's other striker to block the shot.

But after that goal, Virgil went into big game mode. He was determined to get Saints back into the match. In the second half, he pushed forward at every opportunity. It was like his old days as Groningen's emergency extra striker all over again.

Virgil's powerful header was saved and then Oriol Romeu's looping shot crashed against the crossbar.

Was it just Southampton's unlucky day? No, Virgil
stayed in the six-yard box, waiting for the rebound.
It felt like whole minutes passed by as the ball
dropped… down… slowly… onto Virgil's boot. *1–1!*

*Goooooooooooooooooooooaaaaaaaaaaaaaaaaallllllllllll
lllllllllllllllll!!!!!!!!!!!!!!!!!!!!!*

Yes, he had his revenge at last! Virgil ran towards
the Saints supporters with one arm up in the air and a
calm look on his face, like he scored goals every game.

'Let's go and win this now!' Virgil urged his
teammates on. José was on the bench, so he was
proudly wearing the Southampton captain's armband.

Five minutes later, Dušan's dangerous cross from
the left flicked off one Inter defender, then another,
and into the bottom corner. *2–1!*

Southampton were beating Inter Milan! And with
Virgil leading from the back, they held on for another
famous victory.

'Well done, lads, we deserved that!' he cheered at
full time.

Sadly, their Europa League adventure didn't last
much longer, but at least Saints had that one massive

win over Inter Milan to remember forever.

And at least they had Virgil. Because in January 2017, José became the latest Saints star to leave. Not only had Virgil lost his trusty centre-back partner, but Southampton had lost their captain. Luckily, the manager Claude Puel didn't have to look very far to find the club's new leader.

'Virgil will be the new captain of the team,' he announced.

CHAPTER 18

INJURY ISSUES

Could life get any better? Virgil was now the official captain of a Premier League club and he was also one game away from playing in the League Cup final at Wembley Stadium.

'Come on, we've got to get there,' Virgil kept telling his teammates. 'We've worked so hard for this!'

Their semi-final first leg against Liverpool had been one of his greatest games in a Saints shirt. Once Nathan Redmond gave them an early lead, Southampton had lots of defending to do. But Virgil dealt with every danger superbly.

He used his size against Daniel Sturridge,

He used his strength against Adam Lallana,

He used his pace against Philippe Coutinho, and

he used his football brain against Roberto Firmino.

When Virgil played that well, no-one could get past him. The match finished 1–0 – Southampton were so close now.

'Well done, guys,' he walked around the pitch shouting, 'but we're not in the final yet!'

And before that big second leg at Anfield, Virgil and his teammates had a Premier League game to win. It was never easy against a team like Leicester City. They were solid in defence and in attack, they had Jamie Vardy, one of England's best finishers.

In the first half, Southampton looked unstoppable. Virgil kept Vardy quiet, and at the other end, James Ward-Prowse and Jay Rodríguez got the goals. 2–0 – it was looking like the perfect preparation for the Liverpool second leg.

But early in the second half, Virgil tangled with Vardy as he cleared the ball away.

'Arghhhh!' he cried out as he collapsed to the ground.

The striker's studs had caught him on the left ankle. It was an accident, but Virgil was in agony.

He sat there, wincing and waiting for the physio.

'What's wrong?' Ryan Bertrand asked. 'Do you reckon you can run it off?'

Virgil just shook his head. He didn't need to be a doctor to know that it was a serious injury.

The longer he stayed down, the more worried the Southampton fans grew. Uh oh, would their incredible captain be able to continue?

Eventually, Virgil got up and tried to play on through the pain. But it was no use; his ankle was really throbbing now. With a frustrated flail of the arm, he sat down again and started unlacing his boot.

Virgil's game was over, but what about his Wembley dream? The semi-final second leg against Liverpool was only three days away...

'No chance,' the Southampton physio told him straight away. 'I'm sorry, but it's a bad injury.'

Virgil's heart sank. 'How long will I be out for?' he asked, dreading the answer. The final was just over a month away...

'Two months, at least, I'm afraid.'

Two months? There was no way that he would

be fit in time for Wembley!

Virgil had to watch the second leg against Liverpool from the sidelines. It wasn't easy but Southampton did their injured captain proud. The defence stayed strong and in the last minute, Shane Long scored a winner. Saints were through to the League Cup Final!

At the final whistle, Virgil clapped and cheered and tried to keep a smile on his face. He was really happy for his teammates, of course, but he hated not being out there on the pitch with them.

'Don't worry, we'll win the trophy for you!' Ryan promised.

With ten minutes to go, it was still Southampton 2 – Manchester United 2. Virgil could hardly bear to watch as United attacked the Saints goal again and again. Up in the stands, he headed and kicked every ball.

'Keep going!' he muttered under his breath, shaking his restless legs.

But just when it looked like the final would go to extra time, Ander Herrera crossed the ball into the

box and there was Zlatan Ibrahimović, in between
the Southampton centre-backs and completely
unmarked. *3–2!*

Noooooooo! It was a goal that Virgil was sure
that he could have stopped. If only he'd been out
there captaining his team instead of recovering from
injury.

Oh well – hopefully there would be other
opportunities in the future. For now, Virgil had to
focus on getting back to full fitness. Unfortunately,
however, that took much longer than expected.
Two months passed, then three, then four, and
he still wasn't ready to return.

'I can't believe it's taking so long,' Virgil
complained to his mum on the phone. 'At this rate,
I'll probably miss most of next season too!'

It was September 2017 when he finally made
his Premier League comeback, eight long months
after his ankle injury. With Saints winning 1–0 with
five minutes to go at Crystal Palace, the manager
Mauricio Pellegrino brought Virgil on for Dušan to
add some extra calm in defence.

As he ran onto the field, the Southampton supporters let out an almighty cheer. Their captain had returned at last! And even though he'd been out of the team for ages, it was like Virgil had never been away. He was still the same superstar centre-back, with the same speed, strength and great positioning. But before Virgil could really show off his full range of skills, the final whistle blew.

'Ah, it feels good to be back!' he told Ryan with a big smile as they celebrated the victory.

Virgil, however, wouldn't be staying at Southampton for long.

CHAPTER 19

WORLD'S MOST EXPENSIVE DEFENDER

Turning Liverpool into a trophy-winning team was a long-term project for their manager, Jürgen Klopp. The German couldn't just buy all the players that he wanted in one go. That would cause chaos, and besides, the club didn't have that much money to spend. So instead, he had to build his squad up slowly and smartly, summer after summer.

In 2016, Klopp had signed Sadio, Virgil's friend from Southampton, and Gini, his Dutch international teammate.

Then in 2017, Klopp signed Mohamed Salah to play in attack, Andrew Robertson to play at left-back, and Alex Oxlade-Chamberlain to play all over the pitch.

They were all brilliant buys, but there was still one key position that Liverpool were desperate to fill that summer – a star centre-back. They had Dejan Lovren, Joël Matip and Ragnar Klavan, but something was still missing. The team had conceded over ninety league goals in the last two seasons. That was way too many.

'Come on Klopp, we need a star centre-back!' their fans cried out.

What Liverpool needed was a world-class defender, a real leader at the back who could help make everyone around him better. And their manager knew exactly who he wanted.

Klopp had watched Virgil shine so many times, against his Liverpool team but also against AC Milan and Barcelona in the Champions League for Celtic. He really admired the Dutch defender's composure and confidence, as well as his speed and strength. He had it all.

'Virgil's the perfect fit for us,' the Liverpool manager declared. 'We need the best, and that's him!'

But the problem was that he wasn't available at

the right price. During the summer of 2017, it looked certain that Virgil would leave Southampton, either to go to Liverpool or to Chelsea. Both clubs were willing to pay a massive £60 million, but Saints said no. They wanted even more for their incredible captain.

'What?' Virgil responded in disbelief. 'That's not fair – they're making sure that no club can afford me!'

He loved Southampton and he would always be grateful to the club for giving him his first experience of Premier League football. But now, Virgil was ready to take his next step. Liverpool were offering him the chance to play in the Champions League again. He was twenty-six years old; what if he didn't get that chance again?

Earlier that summer, Virgil had travelled to Cardiff with friends to watch the 2017 Champions League Final between Real Madrid and Juventus. As he soaked up the amazing atmosphere and the fantastic football, he had dared to dream that one day, he might still get to play in a big game like that. And as he left the stadium that night, he met a group of Liverpool fans who wanted him to join their club.

Surely that wasn't just a coincidence? It was meant to be!

'I'm sorry but I want to leave,' Virgil told his manager, Pellegrino, firmly.

But Southampton wouldn't budge, and Liverpool didn't have enough money to make a bigger offer. So when the new Premier League season started, Virgil had no choice but to stay where he was. He wasn't happy about it, but he got on with being the club captain. What else could he do? After a long injury, he just wanted to play football again.

Virgil's Liverpool dream wasn't over yet, though. Klopp could have signed another, cheaper centre-back instead, but no, he waited patiently for his first choice. He was building the best squad possible to challenge for all the top trophies. They would just have to find the money for Virgil somewhere, somehow...

In the end, it came from Philippe Coutinho's £130-million move to Barcelona. Once they knew it was a done deal, Liverpool went back with a much bigger, final offer for Virgil, one that Southampton couldn't say no to – £75 million!

Wow, when the new transfer window opened
on 1 January 2018, Virgil would be the new most
expensive defender in the world.

'What a waste of money!' some supporters argued.
'In his last game for Southampton, they let in four
goals. Against Leicester!'

'Yeah, and he's only ever played six games in the
Champions League. For Celtic! Is he really that good?'

Even Alan Shearer wasn't so sure: 'Van Dijk is a
good player, yes, but for £75 million? No, he's not
worth it at all.'

Virgil knew that he had a lot to prove at Liverpool,
but he believed in himself. He always had, even
when he wasn't doing well at Willem II, and when
he got ill at Groningen. Now that he had arrived at
one of the biggest clubs in the world, it was time to
show that he belonged there.

'I'm delighted and honoured to become a
Liverpool player,' Virgil announced proudly. 'I can't
wait to pull on the famous red shirt for the first time
in front of the Kop.'

But what number would he wear on the back of

that shirt? Virgil had chosen '17' at Southampton, but that was already taken. Gini was '5' and Dejan was '6'.

'I'll take 4,' he decided.

That was the number worn by the Liverpool centre-back, Sami Hyypiä. And like Virgil, Hyypiä had also started his career at Willem II. It was meant to be.

From day one, Virgil felt right at home. Liverpool was one big family, like Celtic. He already knew Gini from the Netherlands national team, plus Sadio from Southampton and Andy from his time in Scotland. He also shared an agent with Jordan Henderson. It was meant to be.

Everyone was so friendly! And at the end of Virgil's very first training session, he found a club legend waiting for him.

'Welcome to the greatest team in the world!' Kenny Dalglish greeted him warmly. 'Here's my phone number. If you need anything, just call.'

Virgil wanted to get his Liverpool career started straight away. His ankle injury was gone, and he was raring to go. Their next match was only a few days away. And it wasn't just any old match; it was the Merseyside derby against Everton.

CHAPTER 20

MERSEYSIDE DERBY DEBUT

5 January 2018, Anfield

Virgil was desperate to make his Liverpool debut in the Merseyside derby. It was the third round of the FA Cup rather than a Premier League fixture, but still, playing against their local rivals Everton was always one of the most important matches of the season.

'Hmm, I'm not sure that's a great idea,' Klopp told him. 'You've only just arrived, and you need time to settle in. Look, I'll put you on the bench and we'll see how the game goes.'

Virgil accepted his manager's decision, but suddenly everything changed during the warm-up.

Dejan had a tight hamstring, so he moved to the bench. That meant Virgil would be starting alongside Joël instead.

'Thanks, boss – I'm ready!'

He couldn't wait. Virgil wasn't nervous about his Merseyside derby debut – he was never nervous. He was just super-excited. He gave the 'This is Anfield' sign a quick tap as he walked down the tunnel and out onto the pitch.

Wow, the noise was incredible! It was great to hear 'You'll Never Walk Alone' again, a song the fans also sang at Celtic. Looking up, Virgil could see the red and white of Liverpool all around him – shirts, scarves, flags and banners. And some of them had his name on already! It was a very proud day for him and his family.

'Look, Mum, I made it!' he wanted to shout out. 'Just like I always said I would!'

By the time the game kicked off, Virgil felt calm and focused again. He kept talking to his teammates, pointing and organising them into position. It didn't matter that he was the new kid; it was his job to lead

the Liverpool defence. That's why they had paid
£75 million for him.

It wasn't a perfect performance, but as the game
went on, Virgil grew in confidence. He won his
battles with Dominic Calvert-Lewin and worked
well with Joël. Playing for a top team like Liverpool,
he had more of the ball than ever. It was a fun
chance for him to show off his skills. Most of
the time, he kept his passing pretty simple, but
sometimes, he dared to play long diagonal balls
out to Roberto or Sadio on the wings.

'Excellent!' Klopp encouraged him from the
sidelines.

By half-time, Liverpool were winning 1–0 thanks
to a James Milner penalty. They looked pretty
comfortable, but Virgil knew that he couldn't relax.
He didn't want to make any mistakes, especially
not against Everton. He was aiming to become a
Liverpool hero, not a villain.

Early in the second half, Virgil went up for a
free kick. Although Klopp had signed him for his
defending, he could be dangerous in attack too. At

six-foot four, he was the tallest player in the box.
How amazing would it be if he could score on
his Merseyside derby debut?

Virgil made a late run towards the six-yard box,
watching Alex's cross all the way. It was coming
straight towards him! At the right moment, he
leapt up high and headed the ball downwards.
The power was perfect, but sadly it flew straight
at Jordan Pickford.

'Ahhhhh!' the Liverpool supporters sighed in
disappointment.

'That was your chance and you blew it!' Virgil
scolded himself as he raced back into position.
Hopefully, there was still time left to get another…

But from Liverpool's next corner, Everton
launched a lightning-quick counter-attack. Virgil
and his fellow defenders sprinted back as fast as
they could and managed to stop Phil Jagielka from
shooting. Problem solved? No, because no-one had
spotted Gylfi Sigurdsson's run from deep. Except
Jagielka, who played the ball back for Sigurdsson to
strike first time into the bottom corner. *1–1!*

Virgil was annoyed at himself for following the ball, but most of all, he was furious with his midfielders: 'Why wasn't anyone tracking that run?' he shouted up into the Anfield air.

Virgil could already see that he had lots of work to do if he was going to turn Liverpool into a mean defensive machine. But for now, he had a Merseyside derby to win. Every time he went forward for a free kick or a corner, he was causing problems for the Everton defence. He could feel a goal coming...

However, time was running out for Virgil to become a Liverpool hero on day one. With five minutes to go, he waited in the crowded box for Alex's curling cross. It was another good one and this time, Pickford came off his line to try to punch the ball away. Virgil, however, was much bigger and stronger. He beat the Everton keeper to the ball and steered a glancing header down into the bottom corner. *2–1!*

Gooooooooooooooooooooaaaaaaaaaaaaaaaaalllllllllllll llllllllllllll!!!!!!!!!!!!!!!!!!!!

Anfield exploded with noise and emotion. What a

football fairy tale – Virgil had scored the winning goal on his Merseyside derby debut! He ran towards the corner flag, roaring at the fans, and then slid across the grass on his knees. It was the new greatest feeling in the world.

'Yes, Virg, you beauty!' Alex screamed, wrapping him in a big bear hug.

Soon, Virgil was at the centre of a huge team huddle. At the final whistle, he looked up at the sky with an enormous grin on his face. Debuts didn't get any better than that. Even in his wildest dreams, he hadn't imagined scoring the winner in the Merseyside derby.

As he punched the air with both fists, Virgil thought to himself, 'I've got a really good feeling about playing for this club!'

CHAPTER 21

SO CLOSE IN THE CHAMPIONS LEAGUE

After that amazing Merseyside derby debut, Virgil travelled to Dubai with the Liverpool squad for a warm weather training camp. It was a great chance for him to get to know his new teammates and to adapt to the new team tactics.

At his previous clubs, Virgil had played in defences that dropped deeper and deeper when their opponents were on the attack. There would be no sitting back at Liverpool, though. Klopp wanted his team to press high up the pitch, starting with Sadio, Roberto and Mohamed in attack and ending with Virgil in defence on the halfway line. That way, when they won the ball back, they would be in a better position to counter-attack and score goals.

'I know it feels risky right now,' the manager explained, 'but I believe in you. You read the game so well and even if you do make mistakes, you're quick enough to chase down any striker. And don't forget you've still got a sweeper keeper behind you!'

At first, it did feel a bit dangerous, but Virgil soon got used to Liverpool's high defensive line. It turned out that he was the perfect man for the job – calm, clever and excellent at decision-making. He very rarely got things wrong these days.

'How did you know I was going to do that?' Sadio moaned as Virgil made yet another tackle in training.

He laughed, 'I can read you like a book, mate!'

Virgil was already loving life at Liverpool and soon it was time for his Champions League return. He couldn't wait to hear the anthem again and feel the excitement of the big European nights. That was why he had said goodbye to Southampton and hello to a new life at Liverpool.

With Virgil leading from the back, the team was

on fire. In the Round of 16, they thrashed Porto 5–0 and then in the first leg of the quarter-finals, they beat their Premier League rivals Manchester City 3–0 at Anfield. It was one of the best team performances that Virgil had ever been a part of. Could Liverpool go all the way in the Champions League?

'We can't get carried away,' Klopp warned his players. 'First of all, we need to stay strong in the second leg. City aren't finished yet!'

At Anfield, Virgil didn't have that much defending to do, but he was much, much busier at the Etihad. As soon as the match kicked off, City pushed forward on the attack with Raheem Sterling, Gabriel Jesus, Leroy Sané, Kevin De Bruyne, and David and Bernardo Silva.

Wow, it was going to be a very long night for the Liverpool defence. As Virgil went to clear the ball down the left wing, Sterling rushed in and shoved him over.

'Hey, that's a foul!' Virgil cried out on the floor, but the referee signalled, 'Play on!', and City had the ball.

Uh oh, with their star centre-back out of position, Liverpool were in big trouble. In a flash, Fernandinho passed to Sterling who crossed to Jesus, who was in exactly the place where Virgil would have been. *1–0 to City!*

Virgil waved his arms furiously at the linesman and then the referee. 'No way, that has to be a free kick to us!'

But it was no use; the goal had been given. Virgil had to calm down quickly and focus on stopping City from scoring again.

He won every header against Jesus and Sterling, and every tackle too. He had the speed as well as the strength; that's what made him such a world-class centre-back. And with the pressure on, he always played his best football. The fans trusted him to lead them into the Champions League semi-finals.

In the second half, City pushed further and further forward, looking for another goal. They left big gaps at the back and Liverpool's front three took full advantage.

Mohamed reacted first to a loose ball in the box

and chipped it over the diving defender. *1–1!*

Roberto pounced on Nicolás Otamendi's mistake and slid a shot past Ederson. *2–1!*

Even when Sergio Agüero came on, City still couldn't score past Virgil and the rest of the team. They stood together, united, a strong wall of red shirts. Game over – Liverpool were into the Champions League semi-finals!

Next up: Roma. Liverpool won the first leg 5–2 and, despite some tense moments in the second leg in Italy, they eventually made it through… to the final! Virgil couldn't believe it; in his first half-season at the club, he was going to play in a Champions League Final.

'Bring it on!' he roared.

Liverpool's opponents would be Real Madrid, who had won the trophy for the last two years in a row. It was going to be their toughest challenge yet, but Klopp's players were full of confidence. They had got this far, so why not believe?

'We have nothing to fear!' their manager told them in the dressing room in Kiev. 'We deserve to be here, and when we're at our best, we can beat anyone!'

There would be fascinating battles at both ends of
the pitch.

At one end:

MOHAMED VS SERGIO RAMOS, one of Virgil's
rivals as the best defender in the world. His style was
very different, though; he was all about aggression
and tough tackling.

And at the other:

VIRGIL VS CRISTIANO RONALDO!

He couldn't wait to test himself against one of
the greatest footballers of all time. Just like on his
Liverpool debut, Virgil felt excited, not nervous.

'I wouldn't miss this for the world!'

Whenever the pressure was on, Virgil liked to think
back to his younger days on the Cruyff court in Breda.
Yes, football was about winning, but it was also about
having fun. He played the beautiful game because he
enjoyed it. And although the Champions League Final
was really important, it was just another match. It was
nice to know that there were more important things
in life, especially his wife, Rike, and his daughter, Nila.
Family came first, even before football.

'But I'd really love to lift that trophy!' Virgil thought to himself in the tunnel.

That feeling grew stronger and stronger as he walked out onto the pitch, past the trophy. Yes, he was ready to make his family proud, and all the Liverpool fans too, of course. They held up their red scarves with hope and excitement, bringing the Anfield roar all the way to the Ukraine.

Liverpool! Liverpool! Liverpool!

For the first fifteen minutes, The Reds were on top. The Madrid defenders were really struggling to cope with the speed and skill of Roberto, Mohamed and Sadio. But every time they got a goalscoring chance, their shot was blocked, or saved, or missed the target.

So close! With each wasted opportunity, the Liverpool supporters grew more and more restless in their seats. 'We *have* to take one of these soon!'

If not, Real Madrid had players who could really punish them on the counter-attack...

Ronaldo raced down the right wing at top speed, and into the penalty area. Uh oh, Robbo was out of position, so it was all up to Virgil now. No problem!

Calmly, he jogged over towards Ronaldo, trying to push him as wide as possible.

'Whatever you do,' Virgil kept telling himself, 'don't dive in!'

Just as the Real Madrid striker was about to shoot, he slid in front of him. He didn't manage to block the shot, but he didn't have to. Ronaldo blazed it high over the bar.

'Come on, concentrate!' Virgil urged his teammates. Ronaldo might miss once, but he hardly ever missed twice.

A few minutes later, Liverpool's job became a whole lot harder. Their top scorer Mohamed had to go off with a shoulder injury after an awkward challenge from Ramos. In the stands, some of the fans stood there with their hands on their heads, as if they'd already lost the match.

'Keep going, we can still win this!' Virgil called out as inspiration.

At half-time, the score was still 0–0. Liverpool were playing well; they just had to stay focused and not make any silly mistakes…

It all started with a simple long ball over the top. Virgil jogged back casually, knowing that his goalkeeper would reach it long before Real Madrid's Karim Benzema. The next part, however, was totally unexpected. As Loris Karius tried to throw it out to Dejan, Benzema stuck out a leg and deflected the ball into the net. *1–0!*

Virgil didn't see the first part because he was too busy organising his teammates, but he turned around in time to see the ball roll slowly over the goal line. He stood there, frozen in shock. In all his years of football, he had never seen anything like it. What on earth had just happened?

Ultimately, it didn't matter; all that mattered was that Liverpool were losing and they had forty minutes left to fight back.

'Let's go, let's go!' Virgil encouraged from defence.

With Mohamed missing, who was going to step up and score the equaliser? Virgil was there in the box for the corner, but this time, it was Dejan who headed it goalwards and Sadio who tapped it past the keeper. *1–1!*

'Yes, Sadio!' Virgil screamed as he chased after his friend. Thanks to him, it was game on again!

Unfortunately, Liverpool's joy lasted less than ten minutes. Marcelo crossed from the left and Gareth Bale scored a breathtaking bicycle-kick. *2–1!*

For Virgil, it was another horrible moment where he could only stand still and watch the goal go in, as if in slow motion. It was an unstoppable strike, worthy of winning any football match.

Was there still time for Liverpool to fight back once more? No, but there was time for another bad mistake. Bale hit a swerving shot from thirty yards out and somehow it slipped straight through poor Loris's hands. *3–1!*

Until that moment, Virgil had kept believing. However, as the ball hit the back of the net, he felt his last bit of hope fade away. His head dropped and his shoulders slumped. Liverpool had come so close, they had fought so hard, but ultimately, their 2018 Champions League dream was over.

CHAPTER 22

KOEMAN'S CAPTAIN

It was a long and difficult flight home for the Liverpool players after losing the 2018 Champions League Final. No-one knew what to say – what could they say? It was over and they were all too devastated for words.

Luckily for Virgil, he soon had other football to focus on. Two days later, he was off to Slovakia to play for the Netherlands national team.

Although they had failed to qualify for the 2018 World Cup as well as Euro 2016, things were starting to look a bit better under their new manager, Ronald Koeman. Virgil was delighted to be working with his old Southampton boss again, who had a very special job for him to do:

'I want you to be the new captain of the Netherlands national team.'

Wow, another childhood dream come true! It was the new proudest moment of Virgil's life. There was no greater honour in football than wearing the armband and leading your country.

'Thank you so much, I won't let you down!' Virgil promised.

It felt like the start of a new era for the Dutch team. Old stars like Robin van Persie, Rafael van der Vaart, Arjen Robben and Wesley Sneijder were all gone, and now it was up to the next generation. They had plenty of quality players – Memphis Depay, Quincy Promes, Ryan Babel, Daley Blind, and, of course, Gini and Virgil. It was Koeman's job to get the best out of them and turn them into a winning team, with a little help from his new captain.

The Netherlands could only draw their friendlies against Slovakia and Italy, but their performances were improving ahead of the first-ever UEFA Nations League. When Virgil saw the other two teams in League A Group 1, his eyes lit up:

The new World Cup winners France,

and the Netherlands' big local rivals, Germany.

'Four nice, easy games there!' Virgil joked with Gini.

Yes, they had some tough tests ahead, but that's exactly what the national team needed. The Dutch players couldn't wait to play against Germany in particular. There had been many famous matches between the two countries in the past – at the 1974 World Cup, at Euro 1980, and especially at Euro 1988 when the Netherlands had won 2–1 to make it through to the final. Since then, Germany had won the 2014 World Cup, but as for the Netherlands? They had won nothing.

'They think they're going to thrash us,' Virgil told his teammates, 'but we'll show them!'

Before the Germany game, however, the Netherlands faced France. For Virgil and his brilliant young centre-back partner Matthijs de Ligt, that meant defending against the skill of Antoine Griezmann, the strength of Olivier Giroud... and the speed of the next world superstar, Kylian Mbappé.

'Bring it on!' Virgil declared confidently. He loved
a challenge.

In the very first minute, Mbappé dribbled into the
box and nearly scored. He made up for his near-miss
thirteen minutes later, and scored a goal after a mix-
up in the Dutch defence. Virgil was marking Giroud,
but who was marking Mbappé? It was a question
that no-one could answer.

'Come on, concentrate!' Virgil urged the players
around him. To succeed at international level, they
had to learn their lessons quickly.

After that early error, the Netherlands did improve.
Gini shot just wide, and then Ryan scored an
equaliser. *1–1!*

'Yes, that's more like it!' Captain Virgil clapped
and cheered.

Could they now hold on for the draw? As the cross
came in, Virgil was marking Giroud in the middle
again. He thought he had everything covered, but at
the last second, the French striker snuck in front of
him, stretched out his left leg and volleyed the ball
into the net.

'Nooooooo!' Virgil groaned, turning away in anger. He was supposed to be the team leader now! It was another harsh lesson for him to learn at international level.

Although the match ended in defeat for the Netherlands, there were plenty of positives to take into the next game. The Germans were in for a surprise.

As the match kicked off at the Johan Cruyff Arena in Amsterdam, it was clear that the Dutch players were really pumped up. They were faster to the ball, and fiercer in the tackle.

'Yeahhhhhhhhh!' the fans roared them on.

In the thirtieth minute, Virgil went forward for a Dutch corner-kick. He had scored one international goal already, but that was in a friendly. This was a big game, against their biggest rivals. If he scored here, he would become a true national hero...

Ryan won the header at the back post, but the ball bounced off the crossbar and down inside the six-yard box...where Virgil was waiting to nod it in. 1–0!

Gooooooooooooooooooooaaaaaaaaaaaaaaaaallllllllllll llllllllllllllll!!!!!!!!!!!!!!!!!!!

'Come on!' Virgil shouted passionately as he leapt up and punched the air. It was a moment that he would never ever forget.

That goal gave the Netherlands so much confidence. This time, they were going to win, no matter what. They battled and battled until eventually Memphis and Gini scored to secure the victory.

It was 3–0 against Germany – what a result! Under Virgil's leadership, the Netherlands were officially back in business. With a wonderful 2–0 win over France, they moved to the top of the table. As long as they didn't lose their away game in Germany, they would be on their way to the UEFA Nations League finals…

The Germans, however, were out for revenge. In the first twenty minutes, they stormed into a 2–0 lead. When the second goal went in, Virgil looked around him. He could see that his teammates were losing hope. What could he do? He was the captain of his country now; it was his job to lead the fight-back. Virgil kept talking, organising, encouraging, and pushing his players forward. It wasn't over until it was over. With time running out, Quincy scored a screamer. *2–1!*

'Game on!' Virgil called out. 'Come on, I know we can get another one!' His country was counting on him as captain. Virgil loved the responsibility of his role; it only made him stronger. For the last minutes, he stayed up front as an emergency extra striker, just like in his old days at Groningen. And it turned out that Virgil hadn't lost his scoring touch…

In injury time, Tonny Vilhena curled one last cross into the box. A German defender flicked it on and in a flash, Virgil struck the sweetest volley of his life. The ball flew past Manuel Neuer before he could even react. *2–2!*

Goooooooooooooooooooaaaaaaaaaaaaaaaallllllllllll llllllllllllll!!!!!!!!!!!!!!!!!!!

What an emotional moment! Virgil had helped take the Netherlands national team to the UEFA Nations League finals. He stood in front of the Dutch fans and roared like a lion, like a leader.

'Yesssssss!' Frenkie de Jong screamed out as he jumped on Virgil's back.

Six months later, in June 2019, the team travelled to the final tournament with high expectations. In the semis, hosts Portugal faced Switzerland, while the Netherlands were up against England. For Virgil and Gini, that meant going head-to-head with their Liverpool teammates Jordan Henderson and Trent Alexander-Arnold.

'May the best country win!' they teased each other in the build-up to the game.

After 120 minutes of football, that country turned out to be the Netherlands. Once again, they showed amazing team spirit to fight back, after Matthijs had conceded an early penalty. The Dutch players never gave up; Virgil wouldn't let them.

Matthijs made up for his mistake with a powerful header. *1–1!*

Then in extra time, the Netherlands forced the England defenders into two sloppy errors. *2–1, 3–1!*

Virgil was now just one game away from winning

his first international trophy. And as captain, he
would be the one who got to lift it! That thought
spurred him on as he led the Dutch team out in the
UEFA Nations League Final against Portugal.

It was a re-match of the 2018 Champions League
Final clash – Virgil vs Ronaldo. Who would win
Round Two?

Unfortunately, it was Cristiano's team who came
out on top again. In the sixtieth minute, Gonçalo
Guedes hit a shot that was too hot for Jasper
Cillessen to handle. 1–0! And that turned out to be
the only goal of the game. As hard as they tried, the
Netherlands couldn't quite pull off another comeback.

'Unlucky guys,' Captain Virgil comforted his
teammates at the final whistle. 'Well played – we
gave it everything.'

He was disappointed, but not devastated. After
all, the Dutch had done so well to get past France,
Germany and England to the UEFA Nations
League Final. Along the way, the new Netherlands
national side had proved a lot of people wrong.
Now, Virgil and his talented teammates were

ready for their next major challenge: qualifying
for Euro 2020.

CHAPTER 23

PREMIER LEAGUE PLAYER OF THE YEAR

Back at Liverpool, Virgil was feeling very confident about the 2018/19 season ahead. Over the summer, the club had added what Klopp hoped were the four final pieces of the puzzle that was his best possible squad:

Stoke City's skilful winger Xherdan Shaqiri,

RB Leipzig's box-to-box dynamo Naby Keïta,

Monaco's classy passer Fabinho,

and Roma's sweeper keeper Alisson.

In Virgil's opinion, Alisson was the star signing of the summer. Yes, £55 million was a lot of money for a goalkeeper, but he was worth every penny. Having played against him in the Champions League, Virgil knew that the Brazilian was exactly what they needed: a brilliant shot-stopper, who could also tackle and pass like an outfield player.

Liverpool now had the most expensive defender in the world and the most expensive goalkeeper too.

'No-one's going to get past us now!' Joe Gomez said with a smile during preseason training.

Virgil was like a big brother to him, and a second coach when they were out on the pitch together. He was always talking to him, offering praise and advice. For youngsters like Joe and Trent, Virgil made everything seem so simple and easy.

'That's it – you've just got to read the situation. What's your best option? What's the striker going to do next?'

Virgil liked helping other players to make the most of their abilities. Football was all about working together as a team and he was determined that Liverpool would win something this season. One trophy would be good; two would be great.

The Champions League was top of Virgil's wish-list, especially after losing last year's final against Real Madrid. But he was desperate to win the

Premier League title too. In England, that's what
made you a legend, and becoming a legend was
what playing football was all about.

'Hey, we're definitely good enough to go for both!'
Virgil discussed with Gini.

It certainly looked that way as the 2018/19
season started. Liverpool won each of their first
six league games, scoring fourteen goals and only
letting in two. The first came from an Alisson error,
and the second was an unstoppable strike from
Tottenham's Érik Lamela. Other than that, their
defence looked unbeatable.

Especially Virgil – no-one could get past him. All
Premier League season long, not one single player
managed to get past him. He was so talented that
he could stop every type of attacker:

Speedy ones like Marcus Rashford and Pierre-
Emerick Aubameyang,

Strong ones like Christian Benteke and Glenn
Murray,

Skilful ones like Gerard Deulofeu and Eden Hazard,
and even the sharp-shooting ones like Harry Kane

and Sergio Agüero.

Suddenly, £75 million seemed like a bargain for the best defender in the world!

But Virgil knew that all his hard work would be for nothing, unless Liverpool won a trophy. At the start of January 2019, they were top of the Premier League table and through to the Champions League Round of 16.

'So far so good,' Virgil thought to himself.

It was all going according to plan, but their next opponents, Bayern Munich, would be a tough team to beat. Their Polish Number 9, Robert Lewandowski, was one of the smartest strikers around.

Away at the Allianz Arena, however, Virgil was victorious. Not only did he do his job in defence, but he also assisted the Liverpool attack.

In the twenty-fifth minute, Virgil looked up and spotted Sadio sprinting down the left wing. PING! He delivered a long, perfect pass, straight onto Sadio's right boot. He controlled the ball brilliantly, turned past Neuer and then chipped it over the Bayern defenders. 1–0! Southampton's old stars had done it again.

But with twenty minutes to go, the match was tied at 1–1. There could only be one winner…

As James Milner's corner looped into the Bayern box, Virgil moved into the right position. Then he leapt high off the ground and threw his head bravely towards the ball. BOOM!

Goooooooooooooooooooooaaaaaaaaaaaaaaaaallllllllllll llllllllllllll!!!!!!!!!!!!!!!!!!!!

Scrambling to his feet, Virgil raced over to the cheering Liverpool fans near the corner flag. He was so happy to score another important goal and send his team through to the Champions League quarter-finals.

He's a centre-half, he's a number four,
Watch him defend, and watch him score,
He'll pass the ball, calm as you like,
He's Virgil van Dijk, he's Virgil van Dijk!

One of the great things about him was that the biggest games were his best games. Virgil loved nothing more than playing under pressure.

That was lucky for Liverpool because every game was now a big game. In the Premier League, they had slipped one point behind Manchester City after a series of disappointing draws. The defending wasn't the problem; thanks to Virgil, they were keeping clean sheet after clean sheet. No, now it was the attacking that was the issue.

'Come on, we've got nine games left,' Klopp tried to motivate his players, 'and we have to win them all. Otherwise, the title race is over, and City will be champions again.'

Challenge accepted! Liverpool started scoring goals again and beat Burnley, Fulham and Tottenham.

They couldn't have done it without their star defender, though. With the score at 1–1, Lucas Moura launched a quick Tottenham counter-attack. Uh oh, Virgil was two-on-one against Son Heung-min and Moussa Sissoko.

No problem! In a flash, he read the situation superbly. Sissoko had the ball and he was the player who was less likely to score. So Virgil backed away and let him run forward, while also blocking the path of a pass to Son. As he entered the penalty area, Sissoko had no choice but to shoot himself. *BANG!* He fired it high over the bar.

What clever, world-class defending! And a few minutes later, Liverpool went up the other end and scored the winning goal. It was Virgil, however, who had saved the day in the first place.

'What would we do without you?' Klopp asked at the final whistle, giving his star centre-back a big hug.

Virgil shrugged and smiled. With his manager's help, he had become one of the best defenders in the world. And at the PFA awards ceremony a few weeks later, he was named the new Premier League Player of the Year.

'I'm very proud and honoured,' Virgil thanked the audience, holding the huge trophy in his hands. It wasn't the one he really wanted, though...

The Premier League title race between Manchester City and Liverpool went on and on, and neither team dropped a single point. Every time one of them won, so did the other. It was incredible!

Manchester City 2 Cardiff City 0,
Southampton 1 Liverpool 3,
Crystal Palace 1 Manchester City 3,
Liverpool 2 Chelsea 0,
Manchester City 1 Tottenham 0,
Cardiff City 0 Liverpool 2,
Manchester United 0 Manchester City 2,
Liverpool 5 Huddersfield Town 0…

Virgil refused to give up until the very last minute of the very last match. He scored his team's first goal in a 3–2 win at Newcastle United. Right, the pressure was back on Manchester City now, but two days later, their star centre-back Vincent Kompany scored the winner against Leicester.

'Nooooooo!' Virgil groaned when he saw the scoreline.

The title race went all the way down to the final day in May 2019. Liverpool were at home against Wolves, while City were away at Brighton. If City won, the title was theirs. But if they drew or lost,

Liverpool could lift the trophy instead.

There was a glimmer of hope for Liverpool when Brighton took the lead, but it only lasted for one minute. After that, City stormed ahead – *1–1, 2–1, 3–1, 4–1!*

Despite beating Wolves and finishing with an amazing ninety-seven points, Liverpool would not be crowned the new Champions of England. It was a crushing blow to come so close to winning their first-ever Premier League title. The Anfield crowd still treated the players like heroes, however. What a successful season it had been, their best for nearly thirty years.

'We must be the greatest team to ever finish second!' they all agreed proudly.

Virgil found it hard to believe and painful to accept, but at least his trophy hunt wasn't over yet – because just five days earlier, Liverpool had pulled off another of the greatest comebacks in Champions League history, against Barcelona.

Despite a decent performance at the Nou Camp, the first leg had finished in a 3–0 defeat for

Liverpool. That was largely due to the brilliance of Lionel Messi. Virgil had done his best to win the battle against the Argentinian, but he could create chances out of nothing.

'Look, we didn't deserve that,' Klopp told his disappointed players at full-time. 'But remember, there's still ninety minutes to go – anything could happen!'

Anfield was full of hope as the two teams walked out for the second leg. The Liverpool supporters had seen their club fight back from 3–0 down in the 2005 Champions League Final against AC Milan. They called that 'The Miracle of Istanbul', so why not a 'Miracle of Anfield' now?

The Liverpool players felt positive too, and they showed it by attacking from the start. In the sixth minute, Jordan's shot was saved, but Divock Origi scored the rebound. *3–1!*

'Come on!' Virgil shouted, punching the air passionately. Now, they just needed two more – could they really do this? They had to believe, otherwise what was the point of playing at all?

Even as the minutes ticked by without a second
goal, the players didn't panic. A football match could
change in a flash…

And this one did. Gini came on and scored two
goals in two minutes. 3–3 – Liverpool were level!

Virgil wanted to go wild like the fans above
them in the stands, but no, he had to keep calm.
At the moment, the match was going to extra-time.
And with Messi and Luis Suárez still on the pitch,
Barcelona were always in the game.

At the same time, however, one more Liverpool
goal would take them through to their second
Champions League Final in a row…

Trent was about to walk away and let Xherdan
take the corner, when he suddenly spotted Divock
unmarked in the middle. Surely, it was worth a
try? Trent quickly whipped the ball into the box
and Divock smashed it into the top corner. *4–3 to
Liverpool!* The miracle was complete.

Somehow, despite the deafening Anfield roar,
Virgil stayed calm in defence until the final whistle.
But as soon as it blew, he ran towards Alisson, who

jumped into his arms.

'We did it! We did it!' they shouted again and again together.

Unbelievable – there were no words to describe what they were feeling. It was simply the greatest game that they'd ever played in.

'Right, we really have to win the Champions League after that!' Virgil declared.

And they did. Liverpool were given a penalty in the very first minute in the final against Tottenham. Mohamed stepped up and... scored – *1–0!*

It was simply meant to be. Spurs' strikers tried and tried to score an equaliser, but there was no way past Virgil and Joël. They were too strong, too quick and too clever. Then with time running out for Tottenham, Liverpool went up the other end and scored a second. 2–0 – game over – they were the new Champions of Europe!

For Virgil, it was the perfect end to a sensational season. After overcoming so many setbacks and disappointments during his younger years, he was officially now one of the best defenders – no, one of the best footballers in the world.

Now finally, Virgil had a team trophy to go with all those individual awards – Premier League Player of the Year, PFA Players' Player of the Year, Man of the Match in the Champions League Final… And it wasn't just any old team trophy that he had won; it was the greatest club trophy in the world.

'Can life get any better than this?' Virgil asked himself as he stood there on the pitch in Madrid. He had a smile on his face, a winners' medal around his neck, his orange boots in one hand, and the Champions League trophy in the other.

Despite all that, the answer was still 'Yes!'. Once the excitement wore off, Virgil still had ambitions in his sights: to win the Premier League title with Liverpool, and then to lead the Netherlands to Euro 2020 glory. Was there anything that the Dutch defender couldn't do?

Turn the page for a sneak preview of
another brilliant football story by
Matt and Tom Oldfield. . .

MANÉ

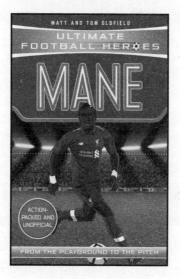

Available now!

CHAPTER 1

EUROPEAN CHAMPION!

1 June 2019, Wanda Metropolitano Stadium, Madrid

'Right, lads,' Jordan Henderson called out from the front of the Liverpool line. 'It's time for us to go out there and win the Champions League!'

'YEAH!' the others cheered behind him. They couldn't lose in the final again – not for a second year in a row! The 3–1 defeat to Real Madrid in 2018 had been so disappointing, but Liverpool had bounced straight back, and this time, they were taking on a team they knew very well – their Premier League rivals, Tottenham.

One by one, the Liverpool players followed their

captain through the tunnel, past the gigantic, silver trophy, and onto the pitch:

Goalkeeper Alisson,

Defenders Joël Matip, Andy Robertson and Trent Alexander-Arnold,

Gini Wijnaldum, Virgil van Dijk, Fabinho,

And finally, the 'Fab Three', the team's star strikeforce:

Roberto Firmino, Mohamed Salah and Sadio Mané.

As Sadio looked up at the thousands of excited faces in the stadium, he could already hear the supporters singing their special song:

We've got Salah, do do do do do do!
Mané Mané, do do do do do,
And Bobby Firmino,
And we sold Coutinho!

The pressure was really on for them to perform, but that didn't bother Sadio. Yes, it was the biggest game of the year, but he was a big game player. He had shown it by scoring in the 2018 Champions

League Final, and on the last day of the 2018–19 Premier League season too. On both occasions, however, Liverpool had failed to lift the trophies they so desperately wanted. Now, in Madrid, Sadio didn't care about scoring; all he cared about was winning.

After beating Lionel Messi's Barcelona 4–3 in the 'Miracle of Anfield', it felt like 2019 *had* to be Liverpool's year to lift the Champions League again. It would be the first time since the 'Miracle of Istanbul' in 2005, which Sadio had watched on TV as a thirteen-year-old boy back in Bambali. But Tottenham, too, had pulled off an incredible semi-final comeback to edge past Ajax. In the final, there could only be one winner.

'And it's going to be Liverpool!' Sadio thought. He was absolutely sure of it.

He had done the Austrian Double with Red Bull Salzburg back in 2014, but since then? Nothing! Sadio was twenty-seven years old now and he couldn't wait any longer. He was determined to collect another winners' medal at last.

A strong start – that's what Liverpool needed,

and that's exactly what they got. After fifteen seconds, Jordan lifted the ball over the Tottenham defence, for Sadio to chase down the left wing…

ZOOM! With that sudden burst of speed, he was away from Kieran Trippier in a flash.

'Go on,' the Liverpool fans urged, jumping out of their seats. 'SHOOT!'

That was Sadio's first thought, but it took a little while to control the bouncing ball. By then, the shooting chance had gone, so what was his Plan B? As he looked up, he spotted Jordan making a late run into the box. But when he tried to chip a pass through to him, it struck the Spurs midfielder Moussa Sissoko on the arm.

'Handball!' Sadio screamed, raising his arm in the referee's direction whereupon Damir Skomina reacted and pointed to the spot. *Penalty!*

What a start – it was still only the first minute of the match! Sadio gave the supporters the signal: 'Make more noise!'

Liverpool! Liverpool! Liverpool!

Another big game, another big-game moment from Sadio. He hadn't scored himself, but hopefully, he had helped his team to take a giant step towards victory...

Mohamed ran up and... scored. *1–0!*

'Come on!' As the other Liverpool players chased after their goalscorer, Sadio sank to his knees and punched the air. Winning any trophy meant so much to him, but especially the Champions League. It would be a childhood dream come true.

There was still a long way to go, however – over ninety minutes of football, in fact.

'Stay focused!' Liverpool's manager Jürgen Klopp called, as he clapped and cheered on the sidelines.

Liverpool expected Tottenham to fight back strongly, but instead, it was Liverpool who had the better goalscoring chances.

As Andy got the ball on the left wing, Sadio skipped between the Spurs centre-backs. He could see the cross coming towards him and he stretched out his right leg... but Hugo Lloris rushed out to make a brave catch.

'Ooooohhhhhhh!' Sadio gasped. *So close!*

Would one goal be enough? With five minutes to go, sub striker Divock Origi finally scored that all-important second. As Sadio watched the ball cross the line, he jumped for joy. Game over; Liverpool were about to be crowned the new Champions of Europe!

Klopp took Sadio off in the ninetieth minute but seconds later, he rushed back onto the pitch to celebrate with his teammates. Virgil, Gini, Trent, Mohamed, Naby Keïta – it was hugs and tears all around!

'We did it,' Sadio cried out as if he still couldn't believe the words. 'We won THE CHAMPIONS LEAGUE!'

First came the winners' medal and then the gigantic, silver trophy. As Jordan lifted it high above his head, the sky was filled with fireworks and loud Liverpool cheers.

Hurraaaaaaaay!

Liverpool! Liverpool! Liverpool!

Campeones, Campeones, Olé! Olé! Olé!

It was easily the best day of Sadio's life so far. It felt like the end of a long and incredible journey, from the dusty streets of Senegal all the way to European football's greatest stage, via adventures in France, Austria and England. Through it all, he had never given up on following his big football dream.

'And look at me now – it was all worth it!' Sadio told himself happily.

He was the top scorer in the Premier League and a European Champion at last. As Sadio walked and danced around the pitch with a Senegal flag wrapped around his shoulders, he couldn't stop smiling. Why? Well, many reasons, but at that moment, Sadio was just imagining the joyful scenes back home in Bambali.

VIRGIL VAN DIJK
HONOURS

Celtic

🏆 Scottish Premiership: 2013–14, 2014–15

🏆 Scottish League Cup: 2014–15

Liverpool

🏆 UEFA Champions League: 2018–19

🏆 UEFA Super Cup: 2019

Individual

🏆 PFA Players' Player of the Year: 2018–19

🏆 Premier League Player of the Season: 2018–19

🏆 Liverpool Players' Player of the Season Award:
2018–19

🏆 Liverpool Fans Player of the Season Award: 2018–19

🏆 UEFA Men's Player of the Year Award: 2018–19

🏆 UEFA Defender of the Season: 2018–19

VAN DIJK

4 **THE FACTS**

NAME: VIRGIL VAN DIJK

DATE OF BIRTH:
8 July 1991

AGE: 28

PLACE OF BIRTH:
Breda

NATIONALITY: Netherlands

BEST FRIEND:
Gini Wijnaldum

CURRENT CLUB: Liverpool

POSITION: CB

THE STATS

Height (cm):	193
Club appearances:	345
Club goals:	37
Club trophies:	5
International appearances:	32
International goals:	16
International trophies:	4
Ballon d'Ors:	0

★ ★ ★ **HERO RATING: 90** ★ ★ ★

GREATEST MOMENTS

30 OCTOBER 2011, FC GRONINGEN 6–0 FEYENOORD

After starting out as an emergency extra striker, Virgil soon settled back into the centre of the Groningen defence. In this Dutch league match, he made a huge impression at both ends of the field. As well as a clean sheet, Virgil also got an assist for a beautiful long pass to Dušan Tadić, and a brilliant long-range goal. It was an all-round performance that the furious Feyenoord manager, Ronald Koeman, never forgot.

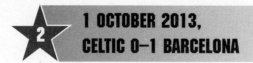

1 OCTOBER 2013, CELTIC 0–1 BARCELONA

At Celtic, Virgil enjoyed his first taste of Champions League football. He raised his game brilliantly against the likes of AC Milan and Barcelona. In this match at Celtic Park, Virgil kept out Andrés Iniesta, Cesc Fàbregas, Pedro, Alexis Sánchez and Neymar Jr for seventy-five minutes. It was the perfect practice for all those big games ahead at Liverpool.

5 JANUARY 2018, LIVERPOOL 2–1 EVERTON

Virgil made his Liverpool debut in this Merseyside derby in the FA Cup. Jürgen Klopp didn't want his new signing to start, but in the end, he had to because of other injured players. Virgil showed no fear as he jumped high to score the winning goal and become an instant Anfield hero. It was a sign of great things to come.

19 NOVEMBER 2018, GERMANY 2–2 NETHERLANDS

In March 2018, Virgil's old Southampton boss Ronald Koeman made him the new captain of the Netherlands national team. It turned out to be a very wise move indeed, as Virgil led his country to the final of the first-ever UEFA Nations League. Along the way, he scored two goals against their rivals Germany, including this late and very important equaliser.

1 JUNE 2019, TOTTENHAM 0–2 LIVERPOOL

It was second time lucky for Virgil in the Champions League Final. A year after Liverpool's disappointing defeat to Real Madrid, he helped lead them to victory over Tottenham. It was skill, rather than luck, however, that helped him keep out Harry Kane and Son Heung-min in the second half. At the final whistle, Virgil also got a second prize to go with his winner's medal: the man of the match award.

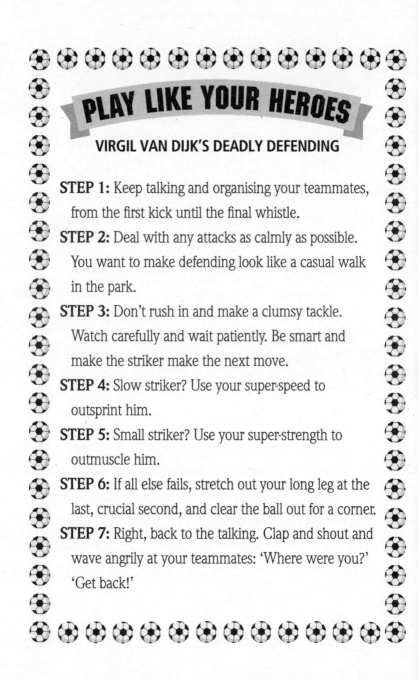

PLAY LIKE YOUR HEROES

VIRGIL VAN DIJK'S DEADLY DEFENDING

STEP 1: Keep talking and organising your teammates, from the first kick until the final whistle.

STEP 2: Deal with any attacks as calmly as possible. You want to make defending look like a casual walk in the park.

STEP 3: Don't rush in and make a clumsy tackle. Watch carefully and wait patiently. Be smart and make the striker make the next move.

STEP 4: Slow striker? Use your super-speed to outsprint him.

STEP 5: Small striker? Use your super-strength to outmuscle him.

STEP 6: If all else fails, stretch out your long leg at the last, crucial second, and clear the ball out for a corner.

STEP 7: Right, back to the talking. Clap and shout and wave angrily at your teammates: 'Where were you?' 'Get back!'

TEST YOUR KNOWLEDGE

QUESTIONS

1. What position did Virgil want to play at his first club, WDS'19?

2. Which Brazilian star inspired Virgil's skills on the Cruyff Court?

3. What was the name of Virgil's local professional club?

4. What job did Virgil do while he played for the Willem II youth team?

5. Why did Virgil have to miss Groningen's big derby match against Heerenveen?

6. How many trophies did Virgil win at Celtic?

7. Virgil was part of the Netherlands' 2014 World Cup squad – true or false?

8. How much money did Southampton pay to sign Virgil in 2015?

9. How much money did Liverpool pay to sign Virgil two-and-a-half years later?

10. Name at least two countries that Virgil's Netherlands team beat in the UEFA Nations League.

11. How many Premier League strikers got past Virgil during the 2018–19 season at Liverpool?

Answers below. . . No cheating!

1. *Striker* 2. *Ronaldinho* 3. *NAC Breda* 4. *He washed dishes at a local restaurant called Oncle Jean.* 5. *He was in hospital, having major surgery on his appendix.* 6. *Three – Two league titles and one League cup* 7. *False – The national team coach Louis van Gaal decided that he wasn't good enough!* 8. *£13 million* 9. *£75 million!* 10. *Any of Germany, France and England* 11. *None!*